Changing Population

Editor: Danielle Lobban

Volume 435

independence
educational publishers

First published by Independence Educational Publishers

The Studio, High Green

Great Shelford

Cambridge CB22 5EG

England

© Independence 2024

ISBN-13: 978 1 86168 895 8

Printed in Great Britain

Zenith Print Group

Acknowledgements

The publisher is grateful for permission to reproduce the material in this book. While every care has been taken to trace and acknowledge copyright, the publisher tenders its apology for any accidental infringement or where copyright has proved untraceable. The publisher would be pleased to come to a suitable arrangement in any such case with the rightful owner.

The material reproduced in **issues** books is provided as an educational resource only. The views, opinions and information contained within reprinted material in **issues** books do not necessarily represent those of Independence Educational Publishers and its employees.

Images

Cover image courtesy of iStock. All other images courtesy of Freepik, Pixabay and Unsplash.

Additional acknowledgements

With thanks to the Independence team: Shelley Baldry, Tracy Biram, Klaudia Sommer and Jackie Staines.

Danielle Lobban

Cambridge, January 2024

Contents

Chapter 1: UK Population

Chapter 2: Global Trends

Introduction

Changing Population is Volume 435 in the **issues** series. The aim of the series is to offer current, diverse information about important issues in our world, from a UK perspective.

About Changing Population

In 2022, the global population reached 8 billion. But is the population rising as rapidly as it has done over the past century? This book explores the aging population and decline in birth rate and how this is impacting the demographic of population.

Our sources

Titles in the **issues** series are designed to function as educational resource books, providing a balanced overview of a specific subject.

The information in our books is comprised of facts, articles and opinions from many different sources, including:

- Newspaper reports and opinion pieces
- Website factsheets
- Magazine and journal articles
- Statistics and surveys
- Government reports
- Literature from special interest groups.

A note on critical evaluation

Because the information reprinted here is from a number of different sources, readers should bear in mind the origin of the text and whether the source is likely to have a particular bias when presenting information (or when conducting their research). It is hoped that, as you read about the many aspects of the issues explored in this book, you will critically evaluate the information presented.

It is important that you decide whether you are being presented with facts or opinions. Does the writer give a biased or unbiased report? If an opinion is being expressed, do you agree with the writer? Is there potential bias to the 'facts' or statistics behind an article?

Activities

Throughout this book, you will find a selection of assignments and activities designed to help you engage with the articles you have been reading and to explore your own opinions. Some tasks will take longer than others and there is a mixture of design, writing and research-based activities that you can complete alone or in a group.

Further research

At the end of each article we have listed its source and a website that you can visit if you would like to conduct your own research. Please remember to critically evaluate any sources that you consult and consider whether the information you are viewing is accurate and unbiased.

Issues Online

The **issues** series of books is complemented by our online resource, issuesonline.co.uk

On the Issues Online website you will find a wealth of information, covering over 70 topics, to support the PSHE and RSE curriculum.

Why Issues Online?

Researching a topic? Issues Online is the best place to start for...

Librarians

Issues Online is an essential tool for librarians: feel confident you are signposting safe, reliable, user-friendly online resources to students and teaching staff alike. We provide multi-user concurrent access, so no waiting around for another student to finish with a resource. Issues Online also provides FREE downloadable posters for your shelf/wall/table displays.

Teachers

Issues Online is an ideal resource for lesson planning, inspiring lively debate in class and setting lessons and homework tasks.

Our accessible, engaging content helps deepen students' knowledge, promotes critical thinking and develops independent learning skills.

Issues Online saves precious preparation time. We wade through the wealth of material on the internet to filter the best quality, most relevant and up-to-date information you need to start exploring a topic.

Our carefully selected, balanced content presents an overview and insight into each topic from a variety of sources and viewpoints.

Students

Issues Online is designed to support your studies in a broad range of topics, particularly social issues relevant to young people today.

Thousands of articles, statistics and infographs instantly available to help you with research and assignments.

With 24/7 access using the powerful Algolia search system, you can find relevant information quickly, easily and safely anytime from your laptop, tablet or smartphone, in class or at home.

Visit issuesonline.co.uk to find out more!

Population growth slowing in all four UK nations, figures suggest

The UK is also continuing to see a long-term shift towards an older population.

By Ian Jones

Population growth slowed in all four UK nations in the decade to 2021, new figures suggest.

Wales is estimated to have seen the lowest growth at just 1.4%, down sharply from 5.3% in the previous decade, while Scotland's population grew by 3.4%, down from 4.7%.

England saw the highest level of growth, with its population increasing by 6.5%, though this was down from 7.4% over the previous 10 years.

Northern Ireland also saw slower growth of 3.4%, down from 4.7%.

Overall, the UK population is estimated to have grown by 5.9% in the decade to June 2021, up 3.7 million to a total of 67.0 million.

This compares with growth of 7.1% in the decade to mid-2011.

The figures have been published by the Office for National Statistics (ONS) and are based on the 2021 censuses for England, Wales and Northern Ireland, along with separate estimates for Scotland, where the census was delayed to 2022.

It is the first time an official estimate has been published for the entire UK population using the latest census data – though the figures will be revised once census information for Scotland becomes available.

The UK population had been increasing at a steadily faster rate in recent decades, with growth of 0.8% in the 10 years to 1981 followed by 1.9% in the 10 years to 1991, then 2.9% to 2001 and 7.1% to 2011.

The latest estimates suggest this pattern has come to a halt, though it is too soon to know if this is a one-off slowdown in growth or the start of a new trend.

The figures also confirm the UK is continuing to see a long-term shift towards an older population, with the median age in June 2021 estimated at 40.7 years, up from 39.6 in June 2011.

Wales had the highest median age in mid-2021 at 43.1 years, up from 41.5 in mid-2011, followed by Scotland at 42.2 years (up from 41.3), England at 40.5 years (up from 39.4) and Northern Ireland at 39.8 years (up from 37.4 – the highest increase).

The ONS said it was not possible to make direct year-on-year comparisons between the new population estimates for June 2021 and those for June 2020.

This is because the figures have been compiled in different ways, with the mid-2020 estimates based on data rolled forward from the 2011 census, while the mid-2021 estimates use the 2021 census.

21 December 2022

Scotland's population growing at lowest rate of any UK nation, census reveals

Country ageing at fastest rate on record and small rise in population due to inward migration, delayed survey shows.

By Severin Carrell

Scotland's population has grown at the lowest rate of any nation in the UK and is ageing at the fastest rate on record, according to the first data from last year's census.

National Records of Scotland (NRS) estimated the country's total population was 5,436,600 last year. Its increase of 141,220, or 2.7%, was driven entirely by inward migration.

Without people moving to Scotland, its population would have fallen by 49,800 since 2011, as deaths outstripped births. By comparison, overall population rose by 6.3% in England and Wales, and by 5.1% in Northern Ireland.

The data, produced after Scotland's census drive last year was hit by high abstention rates, showed the country's population was older than before – a rise partly driven by the post-second world war boom in births.

The number of people aged over 65 was 1,091,000, with a significant proportion of older people living in remote rural areas, often alone.

In Argyll and Bute on the west coast, Dumfries and Galloway, South Ayrshire, the Western Isles and the Borders, older people made up more than 26% of residents. In Glasgow it was 14% and Edinburgh it was 16%.

The Scottish government decided to delay staging Scotland's census by a year until 2022, blaming the Covid crisis, even though the rest of the UK stuck with 2021 as planned. While the census in England and Wales had a 97% response rate, engagement in Scotland floundered, leading to extensions to the response deadlines, warnings that non-responders faced prosecution, and a £140 million total bill.

With response rates particularly low in the poorest neighbourhoods, the Office for National Statistics diverted its Scottish field research staff from ONS projects to help NRS find enough people to go door-to-door to implore householders to fill in the census returns.

NRS confirmed on Thursday that Scotland's overall return rate was 89.8%, which slightly reduced the statistical confidence rate in its figures. To fill in the gaps, NRS used

Scotland's population aged 65 and over has grown by eight percentage points over the past half-century

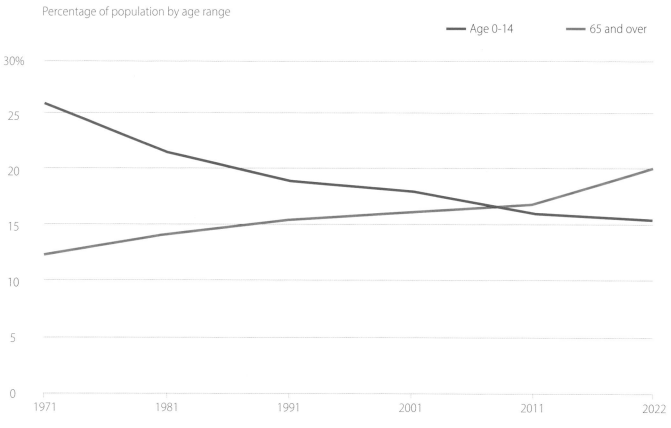

Percentage of population by age range

Age 0-14   65 and over

Source: Scotland's census 2022, 14 September 2023

Scottish borders and rural west have the oldest populations in contrast to urban centres

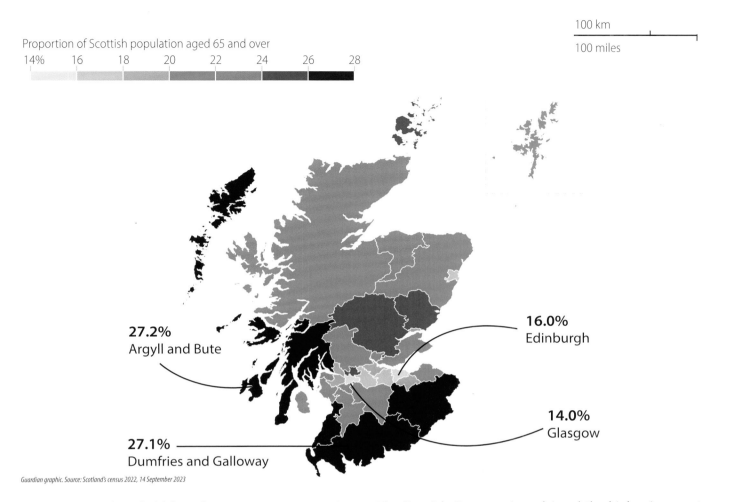

Proportion of Scottish population aged 65 and over

14% 16 18 20 22 24 26 28

100 km

100 miles

27.2%
Argyll and Bute

27.1%
Dumfries and Galloway

16.0%
Edinburgh

14.0%
Glasgow

Guardian graphic. Source: Scotland's census 2022, 14 September 2023

'administrative data' held by other government agencies, such as the NHS and local councils.

Janet Egdell, NRS's chief executive, was asked by an ITV Borders reporter what she believed was behind the low response rate. She initially replied: 'Who knows? Perhaps I shouldn't say that.'

Egdell, who took over as interim chief executive after the decision to delay the census was taken, went on to say it was an 'important question' that would be evaluated after all the data was published. Further detailed releases are due next year.

She confirmed one key question would be whether the next census, due in 2031, would be aligned again with timings in the rest of the UK. Many critics of the Scottish government's decision to delay the census say it contributed to the lower response rates.

Scotland's ageing population trends are made more acute by the lower number of under-15-year-olds in Scotland. For the first time, the number of under-15s has fallen significantly below that of over-65s to 832,600; the number of over-65s in Scotland has risen by 22.5% since 2011.

Economists believe a lower proportion of younger workers increases the financial pressures on governments, because their wealth creation is likely to fall in proportion to the growing cost burdens of supporting an older population.

The Scottish Conservatives claimed the higher income tax rates and public service failures were to blame for Scotland's lower population growth.

Angus Robertson, the Scottish constitution, external affairs and culture secretary, said the population challenges were worsened by Brexit, which made it harder to attract European migrants to Scotland.

14 September 2023

Brainstorm

In pairs, discuss why you think the population is growing slowly in Scotland. Make a list of your ideas.

Voices of our ageing population

Why does population ageing matter and what do the Census 2021 data tell us? This article was compiled in partnership with Age UK, the Centre for Ageing Better and the International Longevity Centre UK.

By Angele Storey

The population of England and Wales has continued to age, with Census 2021 results confirming there are more people than ever before in older age groups. Over 11 million people – 18.6% of the total population – were aged 65 years or older, compared with 16.4% at the time of the previous census in 2011. This included over half a million (527,900) people who were at least 90 years of age.

The average (median) age in England and Wales rose from 39 years in 2011 to 40 years in 2021, reflecting the changing age structure of the population.

This article goes beyond the numbers to provide expert views on issues related to ageing and explain why census data are particularly useful. What do we know about the lives of older people and the challenges they face? How do the data help to plan for an older population? And, what do older people themselves think about ageing and how we could all age better?

> '**Health-wise, I have the odd ache and pain, but I don't feel old. Inside I am still me.**' – Joan Robertshaw, aged 75

Why are data about ageing important?

Angele Storey is head of the Office for National Statistics (ONS) Ageing Analysis team.

She said: 'While living longer is something to be celebrated and our ageing population presents opportunities, it also has implications for the economy, services and society. Knowing the size and structure of the population is fundamental for decision makers and policy makers in the UK. The 2021 Census results will give further insight into the implications of an ageing population and the lives of older people when the more detailed multivariate data are published in 2023.'

The ONS works in partnership with organisations such as the Centre for Ageing Better, Age UK and the International Longevity Centre to ensure that evidence on the UK's ageing population is relevant and helpful.

David Sinclair, chief executive of the International Longevity Centre UK, said: 'For all of the big challenges which come with an ageing population, we are reliant on data to help us to tell the story. The census data give consistency, within reason, over 200 years and also allow us to look to the long term. The census gives really detailed local data, which is extraordinarily important. One of the other advantages for us, is that it is accessible and free.

'Good quality data presented in really clever ways can identify and target interventions better, that can help address inequalities.

'We have done some work that shows if you keep people healthier for longer, they work more, they volunteer more, they care more and they spend more money. You can use data to present solutions.'

Andrew Eastell from Bradford describes himself as 'a young old man'. Now aged 65 years, he used to run a property renting business, which has been taken over by one of his five children.

He said: 'I play walking football on an Age UK team three times a week. I've taken a first aid and coaching course so I can also coach the team. Most of the players are aged over 60 and we have a good laugh and get on really well. I am chairman of an amateur football club and a member of a retro scooter club too.

'I absolutely love getting older. I have so much freedom and time. I'm very fortunate to be as fit as a fiddle and have a good lifestyle. I stopped smoking about five years ago and it was the best thing I ever did. The only thing I miss is playing proper 11-a-side football. I played veterans football up to the age of 60. I know more younger people than older people because of my involvement with football.'

How diverse are older people?

Older people are as diverse as the rest of the population, and it is important not to assume everyone has the same issues and needs simply because of their age.

That is the view of Dr Elizabeth Webb, head of research at Age UK, which provides national and local support and advice to older people, as well as the friendship helpline service Silver Line.

She said: 'Older people don't all fit neatly into convenient boxes and stereotypes. They are enormously varied in terms of their age, health, capabilities, independence, disability, their caring responsibilities, engagement with the labour market, incomes, and the extent to which they're dependent on the state. There are also other diversities like ethnicity, sexual orientation and gender identity. Later life is diverse and complex.'

Later ONS analysis of the 2021 Census data will help show this diversity and the degree to which characteristics of older people have changed or stayed the same over the last few decades.

Joan Robertshaw, aged 75 years, lives in Halifax, has a son and volunteers in a drop-in centre for older people.

She said: 'I worked until I was 64, then volunteered and did lots of things with my husband, Graham. We had some very good times. He died just before Christmas and my volunteer friends have been like a second family.

'The NHS was wonderful when Graham was ill. I was able to look after him myself which I was pleased about; not everyone can do that. I have a really good network of wonderful friends but feel very strongly that I don't want to depend on others, so I am very self-sufficient. I keep busy and occupied and I am getting on with my life.

'Health-wise, I have the odd ache and pain, but I don't feel old. Inside I am still me. I think a lot of older people worry about what happens if they end up on their own or what if they can't manage on their own or financially manage. I take each day as it comes and if I can make someone laugh or if someone is pleased to see me, that's good enough for me.

'Older people are just people who have lived longer than others. If you are fortunate you will live to be an older person as well. I am thankful for the life that I have had and for my family and friends.'

What are the challenges of ageing?

The Centre for Ageing Better was launched in 2015. Dr Aideen Young, Senior Evidence Manager at the Centre, highlights some of the challenges facing older people.

She said: 'Older people are a highly diverse group in terms of health and wealth, and within that group there are people very much in need – who are living in poverty, in poor housing and in poor health. Their precarious situation has been exacerbated by the cost of living crisis. They are the people that we really need to pay attention to.

'We have the oldest housing stock in Europe so there are many people living in non-decent and inappropriate homes. These homes are simply not suitable for people who are older or who have disabilities.'

Age UK's Dr Webb said: 'Our responsibility at Age UK is to be there for the older people who need us. We know there are an awful lot of older people who don't need us. There are plenty of people aged over 65 who are in great health, have excellent incomes and good housing. Everything is working well for them. These people often are our volunteers or donors but at some point, later in their life, they may become our service users.'

> **'I am blessed to be able to move about and do the things that I want to do. Losing my independence would really bite into me.'**
> – Zafar Kayani, aged 65

Analysis of 2021 Census data will give us the most up-to-date, detailed picture of the differing circumstances of older people living in England and Wales.

David Sinclair said that one of the main challenges of an ageing population is how to support people to age well.

He said: 'We start ageing in the womb so we need to be looking at the young. We need to be thinking about access to education and learning across the whole life so that we can make sure we are prepared for the 100-year life, even if that doesn't end up being everyone. We also need to change the narrative and debate around supporting people to work longer. We need to address challenges like pensioner poverty, shortages in housing and inequalities in health and life expectancy.'

Dr Young echoed this theme. She said: 'At the Centre for Ageing Better, we have primarily focused on people in mid-life because by creating change for people in this age group

we can enable them to have a good later life when they get there.'

Census data provide a snapshot in time of the characteristics of people of all ages. A 1% sample of census records are also linked through the once-per-decade censuses back to 1971 in the ONS Longitudinal Study. These data - together with events data including deaths - allow researchers to examine changes in people's attributes and socio-demographic characteristics as they age.

David Sinclair said the UK had been ageing very slowly when compared with places such as South Korea, Hong Kong or Singapore.

He said: 'That also means our society has been a bit slower to adapt. We need to use the data we have to plan better for the future.'

Dr Webb added: 'If we had more accessible public transport and public toilets this wouldn't just be good for older people, it would help people on lower incomes, people with disabilities, and parents and children too. A lot of our interests align.'

Angele Storey said a census provides one of the best sources of data for planning:

'It can also be combined with administrative-based data or survey data to build a greater understanding of complex populations and their needs,' she added.

Zafar Kayani is 65 years old and lives in Bradford. He has three sons, four grandchildren and works full-time in community engagement for a voluntary group for dads and young children. He is also a yoga teacher.

He said: 'When I was younger, I thought 65 was a long way away but now I have reached that milestone, it didn't take that long. Being older does mean you get a lot more respect from other people. It reminds me I am an old man when people call me uncle.

'I am blessed to be able to move about and do the things that I want to do. Other people my age or older may not be as mobile and need to rely on other people. Losing my independence would really bite into me.

'To keep well, it's important to have the opportunity to talk to other people and socialise in groups. Keep your mind and body active. You tend to have more time when you are older and can lose focus, so you need to create things to focus on.

'I started a walking group in my local area about a month ago. After we walk, we have tea and biscuits and talk. The youngest person in the group is 50 and the oldest is 85. They say it has given them a purpose and something to look forward to. They feel part of something. You should celebrate what you have got and enjoy life.'

'I absolutely love getting older. I have so much freedom and time.' – Andrew Eastell, aged 65

Which areas have the oldest populations?

Census data help the Centre for Ageing Better identify where the most aged and most rapidly ageing communities are in the country.

Across England and Wales, 2021 Census data showed that the local authorities with the highest proportions of older residents in their populations tended to be either or both rural and coastal areas. North Norfolk had the highest, where a third of residents (33.5%) were aged 65 years and over. Rother had the next highest percentage at 32.4% followed by East Lindsey at 30.4%. The three local authorities that have seen the largest increase in the percentage of their population aged 65 and over since 2011 were Richmondshire, Derbyshire Dales and Hambleton.

The local authorities with the lowest proportions of residents aged 65 years and over were the London boroughs of Tower Hamlets (5.6%), Newham (7.2%) and Hackney (7.9%).

Dr Young said: 'However, it's not enough just to know where the older people are because of course it also matters whether they are ageing well in those places. We are also looking forward to the coming census data, at both a national and local level, that tells us about other aspects of people's lives, for example, their health and the number living alone. We also look forward to data on the numbers of older people from ethnic minority communities because we know there is enormous inequality in how they experience ageing. We need to know the numbers to be able to know where action is needed; we need the numbers to present to policy makers and that's why the census data is so vital for us.'

Lizzie Gent, aged 64 years, lives in Manchester and is a part-time librarian and volunteer. She moved to half-time working in 1997 to look after her partner Marion who had multiple sclerosis. She died around eight years ago.

> ## 'It is important to acknowledge that older people have lived fascinating and interesting lives and have individual stories to tell.' – Lizzie Gent, aged 64

Lizzie said: 'Like many people who lose a partner, I had to build another life after she died and become someone different.

'That's when I started volunteering and I also joined a choir. I am now chair of the choir committee. I cycle a lot and do a fitness routine at home some mornings. I hope I am going to carry on cycling into my 90s.

'Most of my friends are my age and are fit and active. I am also surrounded by really positive older women in their 70s. Some live with things like arthritis or other aches and pains. My mum is aged 99 and lives in a care home. I am very aware of other friends who are struggling to pay for their elderly parents' care.

'To keep healthy and live longer I would advise people to keep active, maintain a good group of friends and do an activity that brings you into contact with people like singing or volunteering. Seek out new experiences and learn new

Key Facts

- Census 2021 revealed over 11 million people – 18.6% of the total population – were aged 65 years or older, compared with 16.4% at the time of the previous census in 2011. This included over half a million (527,900) people who were at least 90 years of age.

- The average (median) age in England and Wales rose from 39 years in 2011 to 40 years in 2021, reflecting the changing age structure of the population.

- Across England and Wales, 2021 Census data showed that the local authorities with the highest proportions of older residents in their populations tended to be either or both rural and coastal areas. North Norfolk had the highest, where a third of residents (33.5%) were aged 65 years and over.

- The local authorities with the lowest proportions of residents aged 65 years and over were the London boroughs of Tower Hamlets (5.6%), Newham (7.2%) and Hackney (7.9%).

skills. Try to enjoy life as much as possible and go out into the countryside.

'People often have an image of older people as an amorphous bunch. It is important to acknowledge that older people have lived fascinating and interesting lives and have individual stories to tell.'

Dr Young encouraged people to think about the fact that they are going to get older themselves.

She said: 'Ageism is discrimination against your future self and that makes no sense.'

2 November 2022

Write

Write a definition of Ageism.

Consider...

Why are rural and costal areas more likely to have an older population?

What effects can an ageing population have on an area?

How can the Government prepare for an ageing population? What policies might need to be introduced to prepare for a future with an elderly population?

The impact of migration on UK population growth

Based on official population estimates and population projections, this briefing examines the impact of migration on recent and future UK demographic trends.

Key points

- More than half (60%) of the increase of the UK population between 2001 and 2020 was due to the direct contribution of net migration.

- Official figures project that the growth in the UK's population will be slower over the next 25 years than in the previous 25 years. The UK's population is projected to grow to approximately 72 million by 2045.

- Scotland and Wales would experience population decline without future net migration.

- Net migration assumptions have been continually revised in the projections released since the mid-1990s, reflecting rising levels of net migration and the high uncertainty of migration forecasting.

Understanding the evidence

Key concepts

In the UK statistical system, long-term international migrants are defined as people who move into and out of the country for at least 12 months. Net migration is the balance between immigration and emigration over a given time period. In demographic terms, natural change – i.e. the difference between the number of births and deaths – measures the contribution of vital events to the dynamics of the population. Immigration and emigration contribute to population change not only by altering the number of individuals in the country at a given time (direct contribution) but also by affecting natural change (indirect contribution).

Population estimates

The Office for National Statistics (ONS) produces annual estimates of the resident population of England and Wales and estimates for the UK as a whole by collating data provided by the Northern Ireland Statistics and Research Agency (NISRA) and by the National Records for Scotland (NRS). The population at 30 June of a given year (stock) is obtained by annually 'updating' the most recent census population count with data on demographic events contributing to population change between these two dates (births, deaths and migration flows). Population estimates made between census years are revised retrospectively so as to provide a consistent series of population estimates over time. For example, the revised estimates for the period between the 2001 and 2011 censuses resulted in an adjustment of 497,500 (0.8%) largely due to the underestimation of net migration in the previous series. Mid-year population estimates are also used as the base-year population of demographic projections.

Population projections

Population projections are calculations showing the future development of a population based on a set of assumptions about fertility, mortality and net migration. Official UK projections are usually revised every two years by updating base-year population estimates and assumptions underlying future demographic dynamics so as to reflect the latest available information. The Covid-19 pandemic disrupted the usual schedule and publications, however.

The most recent full set of projections–including variants to assess the impact of higher or lower net migration–used mid-2018 as the beginning of the projection period. In these projections, ONS provides a principal projection reflecting the most 'likely' population developments on the basis of recently observed trends, and a number of variant projections, intended to capture the uncertainty of the assumptions by showing the impact on population dynamics if one or more components of demographic change differ from the principal projection. For comparative purposes, an important variant projection is 'zero net migration' (aka 'natural change only'), which assumes migration inflows and outflows exactly equal at all ages throughout the projection period (with same fertility and life expectancy as the principal projection). In this scenario, future population change is driven only by births and deaths. The comparison between the principal projection and the zero net migration variant allows one to assess the overall impact of net migration on population trends – i.e. Including both the direct contribution and its impact on natural change.

In 2022, the ONS published updated projections based on 2020 data, but did not include any variants. It then updated this 2020-based projection in light of unexpectedly high net migration estimates, publishing a new projection in January 2023. This most recent principal projection assumes that net migration will level off at 245,000 per year from 2026-7 onwards. This figure represents the estimated 22-year average net migration preceding the most recent projection. The net migration assumption was increased from 205,000 per year in the previous projection that was published in January 2022, following an ONS review of its methodology.

Net migration exceeded natural change for most of the past two decades

Population estimates show that net migration was a major component of population growth over the past two decades (Figure 1), making up 60% of population growth from 2001 to 2020. Natural change – i.e. the difference between the number of births and deaths – has remained positive throughout the last two decades, but has fallen since 2011.

This retrospective analysis does not account for the contribution of past migration to natural change – mainly to births. The number of births over a given period is determined both by the size and age structure of the female population and by fertility rates (i.e. the average number of

Figure 1

Annual population change

Contribution of net migration and natural change: 1992-2020

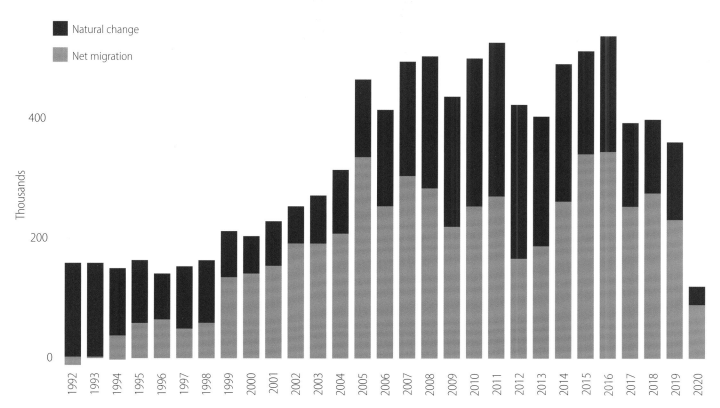

■ Natural change

■ Net migration

Source: Office for National Statistics, mid-2020 population estimates

children per woman in each age group). Migration affects both. That is, it affects the number of women of childbearing age and, if migrant women have different fertility patterns, the total fertility rate of the population as a whole. ONS figures show that in 2021, 28.8% of births in the UK were to non-UK born mothers. This is higher than the share of non-UK born people in the UK population, primarily because non-UK born women are more likely to be of childbearing age. The estimated total fertility rate of foreign-born women living in the UK has declined over the past 10 years to just below 'replacement rate', and stood at 2.03 in 2021. This compared to 1.54 for UK-born women. Note that these figures include non-UK born women regardless of how long they have lived in the UK.

The UK population is projected to grow to approximately 72.4 million by mid-2045

The most recent population figures from the Office for National Statistics projected that the UK population would grow to 72.4 million by mid-2045. They assumed that net migration would average 245,000 in the long term, starting from mid-2027, i.e. a decline from the unusually high net migration levels seen immediately after the pandemic. The projected rate of growth in the coming 25 years (5.4 million or 8.0%) was slower than the rate of growth seen in the previous 25 years from mid-1995 to mid-2020 (9.1 million or 15.6%). Under this projection, the UK population would reach 70 million by mid-2031.

Figure 2 shows how sensitive the projected size of the UK population is to different assumptions about net migration.

It does this by using the earlier, 2018-based ONS projections, which included variant projections for different levels of net migration. After 25 years, the UK population would be 9% lower if net migration was zero, compared to the 2018-based principal projection which put net migration at 190,000 per year. Under the high migration variant (i.e. 290,000 per year), the UK population would be 4% higher than if net migration had averaged 190,000.

The projected population increase from the 2018-based projections can be broken down into three components: the natural change that would occur in the absence of net migration during the projection period (zero net migration variant); the direct contribution of post-2018 net migration (i.e. the number of individuals who will migrate to the UK minus the number of those who will leave the country); and the indirect contribution of post-2018 net migration, i.e. its effect on natural change.

The UK population was projected to rise both because of positive natural change and because of positive net migration. However, in the absence of further net migration, ONS projected that natural change (i.e. births minus deaths) would be negative after 2028, and that by 2043, the population would slightly decline.

In the principal projection, the cumulative net inflow of new migrants after 2018 accounted for 73% of total population growth by 2028, and 84% by 2043. If one also includes in the calculation the impact of future migration on births and deaths, the total contribution of migration (direct plus indirect) is slightly higher, at 79% by 2030 and 86% by 2045.

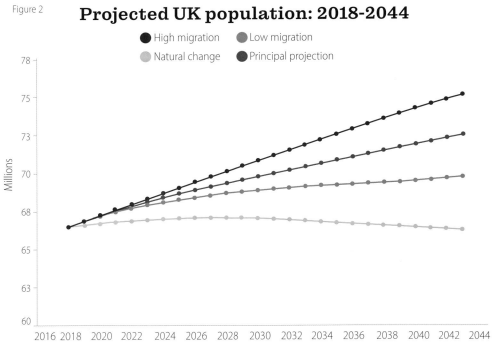

Figure 2
Projected UK population: 2018-2044

● High migration ● Low migration
● Natural change ● Principal projection

Source: Office for National Statistics, 2018-based population projections

To understand the impacts of net migration, we must return to the 2018-based population projections (Figure 3). In England and Wales, net international migration was projected to make the largest contributions to population change by 2043 (+ 8% and +5%, respectively). Scotland would experience considerable population decline (-8%) in the absence of net international migration or 'cross-border migration' from other parts of the UK, and it is also the nation that receives the highest percentage population growth as a result of net cross-border migration. In contrast, in Northern Ireland (which has the highest fertility rate amongst UK nations), natural change without net migration is projected to be the main driver of future population trends (+4%).

Scotland and Wales would experience population decline without future net migration

Demographic and migration trends differ considerably across the four UK constituent nations, and future population scenarios reflect these differences. According the ONS principal projection published in January 2023, England would experience the fastest population growth, at 9% over the next 25 years. Wales and Scotland were projected to have slower rates of increase, at 5% and 1% respectively.

Evidence gaps and limitations

Population projections are not forecasts. They do not attempt to predict the impact of changes in the political, economic, social and cultural realm which may affect demographic patterns and trends. They are usually purely mechanical calculations that show the outcomes of sets of assumptions made for the three components of demographic change (fertility, mortality and migration). Projections are typically reliable for the short to medium term, with the exception of periods of shock such as the Covid-19 pandemic. Uncertainty

Figure 3
Drivers of projected population growth, UK nations, 2018-2043

% of initial population

England   Scotland   Wales   Northern Ireland

■ Natural change (zero net migration)
■ Natural change (due net migration)
■ Net international migration
■ Net cross-border migration

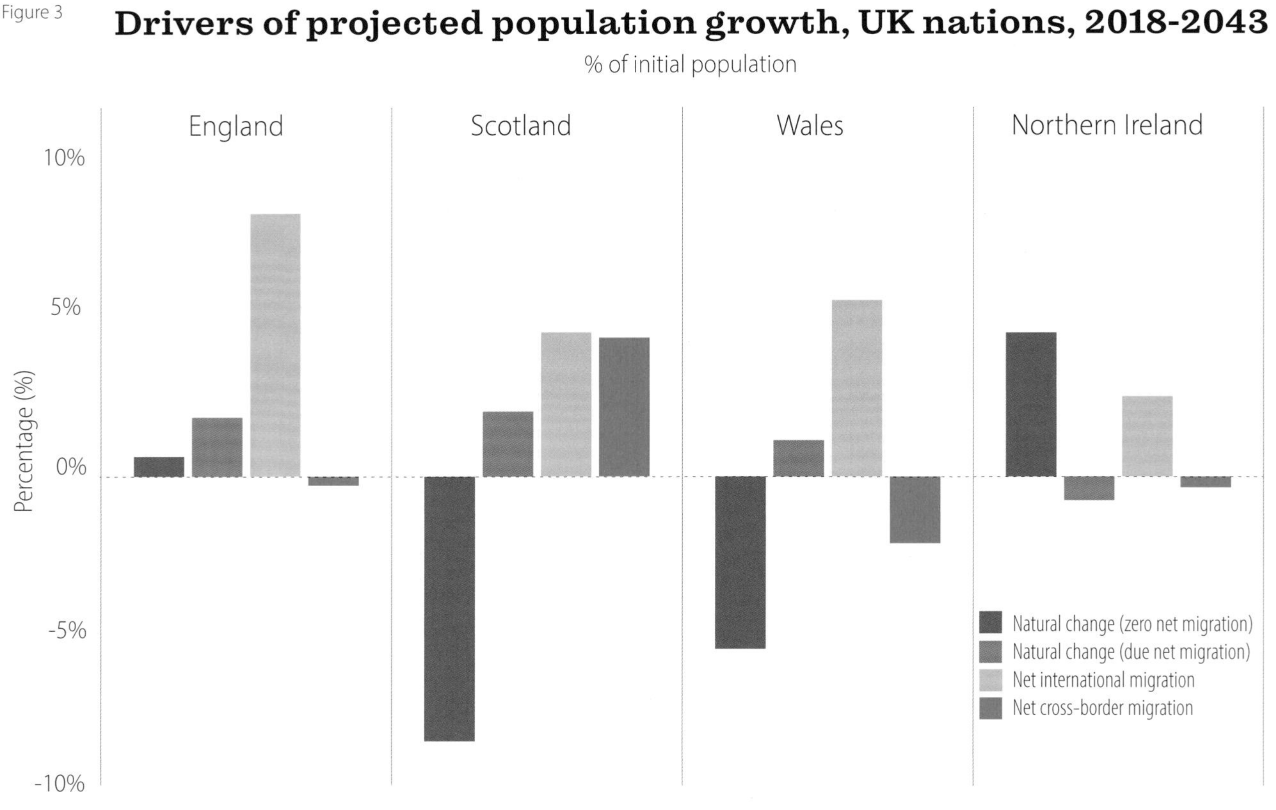

Source: Office for National Statistics, 2018-based subnational population projections

Figure 4

Projected UK population, principal variant

Selected base years, 1994-2020

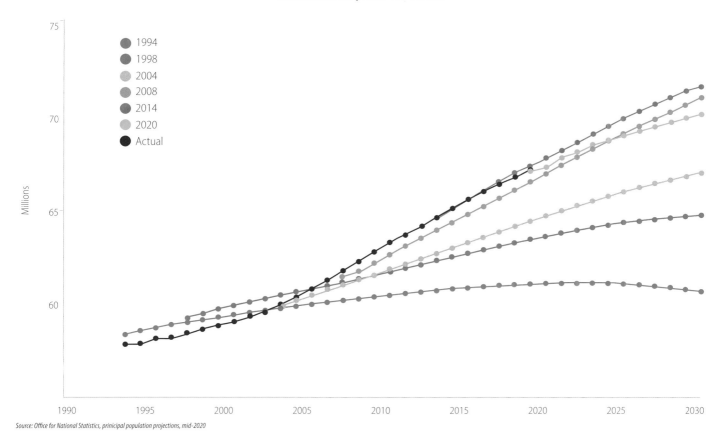

Legend:
- 1994
- 1998
- 2004
- 2008
- 2014
- 2020
- Actual

Y-axis: Millions

Source: Office for National Statistics, prinicipal population projections, mid-2020

increases the further the projections are carried forward in time. Any upward or downward changes in fertility, mortality and migration assumptions, compounded over time, can lead to significant variations in the projected population size and structure.

Future international migration is more difficult to project than fertility and mortality because migration flows are often affected by sudden changes in economic, social, or political factors which are hard to predict or quantify – as exemplified by the sharp increase in net migration in 2021-2022 following the war in Ukraine and the emergence from the Covid-19 pandemic. Migration assumptions are therefore the major source of uncertainty for long-term population projections, particularly in demographic regimes such as the UK which are characterised by below replacement fertility and low mortality levels.

In order to reflect the information provided by the most recently observed demographic trends, assumptions of future levels of fertility, mortality and migration are continually updated in subsequent revisions of population projections. This has resulted in sizeable revisions in different sets of population projections released throughout the 1990s and 2000s. In the 1994-based principal projection net migration was assumed to return to zero in the long-term, reflecting the balance between immigration and emigration proximate to zero observed during the 1980s and early 1990s. As a result, the size of the UK population was projected to peak at 61 million in 2023 and then start to decrease (Figure 4).

In the subsequent sets of projections, upward revisions of assumed net migration levels were introduced to reflect the rapid increase in migration flows to and from the UK. As a result, projected population growth rates have also increased. In the latest revision (2020-based, published January 2023) the projected size of the UK population in 2031 was around 9 million higher than in projections produced in the mid-early 1990s.

The ONS does not attempt to model the impact of policy changes when setting its migration assumptions, and thus current projections do not reflect a prediction about how current policy will affect future net migration.

27 February 2023

Acknowledgement:
Thanks to Zachary Strain-Fajth and Mihnea Cuibus for research assistance with the 2023 update of this briefing.

www.migrationobservatory.ox.ac.uk

UK birth slump dubbed 'good for planet' as number of babies born hits 20-year low

Birth rate slump in West will address overconsumption, former government adviser says.

By Eir Nolsøe

Britain's top demographics expert has said the falling number of babies born in Britain is a 'good thing' after new data showed the number of births had hit a 20-year low.

Professor Sarah Harper CBE, founder and director of the Oxford Institute of Population Ageing and a former government adviser, said falling birth rates in the West were 'good for... our planet'.

Her comments came after official figures from the Office for National Statistics (ONS) showed there were 605,479 live births in England and Wales last year, the lowest number since 2002.

The total was down 3.1 per cent compared to 2021 and is part of a long-term decline in the number of births across Britain and the developed world.

Prof Harper told the *Telegraph*: 'I think it's a good thing that the high-income, high-consuming countries of the world are reducing the number of children that they're having. I'm quite positive about that.'

The academic said declining fertility in rich countries would help to address the 'general overconsumption that we have at the moment', which has a negative impact on the planet.

Prof Harper served on the Prime Minister's Council for Science and Technology between 2014 and 2017. She was awarded a CBE for services to demography in 2018.

She said the UK's declining birth rate was 'inevitable' and in-line with trends in other developed economies.

She said: 'We will see smaller populations in high-income countries going forward. It's just going to be a trend of the 21st century and that will actually be good for general overall overconsumption that we have at the moment and our planet.'

Research has found that wealthy nations tend to have much larger carbon footprints than poorer countries, as rich people can afford to buy more goods, travel more and do other activities that generate emissions.

Carbon emissions from high-income countries were 29 times larger than low-income countries on a per capita basis in 2020, World Bank figures show.

Number of babies born slumps to 20-year low

Number of live births in England and Wales

Source: ONS

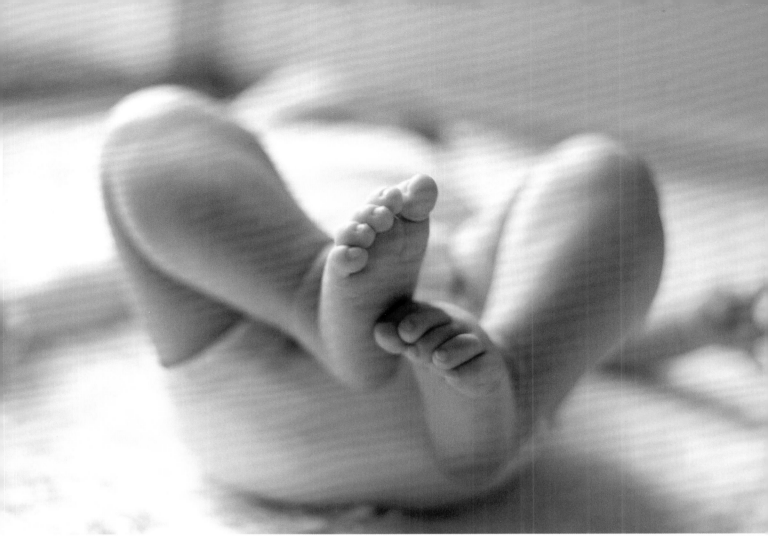

While slowing population growth may reduce carbon emissions, analysts have warned that it also poses significant challenges for economic growth.

A shrinking workforce puts pressure on younger generations to pay more tax for the healthcare of older people. It can also lead to worker shortages that can slow growth.

While the overall number of births in Britain is declining, the share of children born to women from outside of Britain has hit a record high.

Almost one in three children born last year were delivered by mothers born outside of the UK. The number of births by women born outside the UK rose 3,600 year-on-year to account for 30.3 per cent of all births. The previous peak was 29.3 per cent in 2020.

When including the father, more than one in three children born last year had at least one foreign-born parent. In London, the figure was two thirds.

The ONS said: 'In 2022, India replaced Romania as the most common country of birth for non-UK-born mothers, and Pakistan as the most common country of birth for non-UK-born fathers.'

For the first time since records began in 2003, Afghan women were among the top ten most common nationalities for foreign-born mothers.

It comes after Afghan women were granted humanitarian protection by the UK following the Taliban's return to power in 2021.

The number of births is separate from Britain's fertility rate, which measures the ratio of live births to women of childbearing age. This will be published later in the year, as population estimates for mid-2022 are yet to be released.

The fertility rate sank to a record low of 1.58 children per woman during the first year of Covid and recovered slightly to 1.61 in 2021.

17 August 2023

Key Fact

- Official figures from the Office for National Statistics (ONS) showed there were 605,479 live births in England and Wales last year (2022), the lowest number since 2002.

Brainstorm

In pairs create a diamond 9 chart to list the factors that contribute to a falling birth-rate.

Encouraging population decline is pure defeatism

By Matthew Lesh

- There's ample evidence that as cities get more dense they become more innovative and productive

- Lower birth rates and higher life expectancy will create a £250 billion hole in public finances by the mid-2070s

- Extolling the benefits of population decline is straight out of the anti-growth coalition playbook

A new academic paper arguing that a declining birth rate may actually boost living standards has grabbed some attention in recent days. Professor David Miles – who happens to be the chief forecaster for the Office for Budget Responsibility (OBR) – contends that 'the economic impacts are likely, on balance, to be positive' from falling populations.

Miles argues that a smaller population can increase the average quality of life because a higher population puts strains on limited public services, infrastructure and housing. A smaller population also means that less needs to be saved and invested, and more can be spent on consumption today.

This idea is superficially attractive – the country is full, we can't build anything, and thus fewer people would be a good thing. 'The UK appears collectively unable to save enough to stop its infrastructure (public and private) falling behind,' Miles says while referring to 'the anecdotal evidence from

just looking at the UK's crowded roads, trains and ever-shrinking houses'.

There is a marked defeatism at the heart of Miles' argument. Britain's lack of investment is taken as given – rather than a policy choice of successive governments. Miles is effectively playing with a new form of Malthusian logic, that is to assume the economy resembles a fixed structure, rather than something that can be expanded.

Indeed, as is pretty much universally acknowledged, the UK is facing a low-growth crisis. But there is nothing inevitable about this predicament. There isn't a lack of willingness to invest in housing or infrastructure, there is a lack of permissions from the state because of a broken planning system. As Sam Dumitriu and Ben Hopkinson from Britain Remade recently pointed out, railways, trams, and roads cost significantly more to build in the UK compared to elsewhere because of NIMBY power and excessive bureaucracy.

The great human advancements of recent centuries have come from the ability of large populations to specialise, and identify and nurture exceptional talent. A smaller population practically means we are less likely to identify the next Einstein or have someone like Elon Musk who is able to build a company on the way to make us a multiplanetary species. We may just miss out on the next Steve Jobs, who brought communications and entertainment to our pockets.

But it's not just exceptional talent we lose. There's ample evidence that as cities get more dense they become more innovative and productive – a phenomenon known as amalgamation effects. When populations decline, these benefits disappear or can even go backwards.

Matt Ridley in the *The Rational Optimist* points to the case of Tasmania: a striking case of technological regress. Humans reached Tasmania at least 35,000 years ago, but rising sea levels cut off the island around 10,000 years ago. Isolation and declining population numbers meant there was not enough manpower to sustain tool kits and lifestyles. 'The first Tasmanians caught and ate plenty of fish, but by the time of Western contact they not only ate no fish, , but had not eaten any in over 3000 years' Ridley writes, in one of many examples of regress.

The other issue of a declining population that is particularly important considering Miles' employer, is the pressure on public budgets. Indeed, the OBR estimates that lower birth rates and higher life expectancy will create a £250 billion hole in public finances by the mid-2070s.

An ageing population means fewer workers being forced to pay higher taxes to fund pensions, health and social care. We are already seeing early signs of these issues as many have not returned to the workforce after Covid, causing labour shortages, while taxes and spending have risen to post-war highs.

Miles' solution to this is to 'expect some continued labour force participation' and 'a fundamental rethink about the pattern of careers'. So, expect older people to work longer. This is a good and justifiable idea. But it is already proving

extremely difficult to achieve, particularly as a generation of well-off propertied baby boomers comes into retirement and have little direct financial incentive to keep working (as well as a triple-locked pension and increasingly generous social care).

At one point, Miles criticises sharp rises in fertility and high levels of immigration partly on the basis that the UK is a densely populated country. This in itself is hogwash. In fact, just 6% of land in the UK is within urban areas, much of which is made up of gardens and parks.

Interestingly, Miles also does not bother to analyse the economic impact of immigration. Study after study finds that immigrants are disproportionately likely to start entrepreneurial companies, contribute to public revenues and bring necessary skills – including in construction and health and social care. It's hard to see the UK maintaining its quality of life without these immigrants.

It's small-minded to conclude that the UK should forgo population growth because we cannot invest enough. It would just mean capitulating to the forces of managed decline, higher taxes on fewer workers, crumbling public services, and a less dynamic society. The anti-growth coalition must be rejected.

14 September 2023

Matthew Lesh is Director of Public Policy and Communications at the Institute of Economic Affairs.

Columns are the author's own opinion and do not necessarily reflect the views of CapX.

Write

Write a short definition of each of the following:

- Population
- Overpopulation
- Depopulation

Consider...

What are some of the issues with an ageing population?

What causes a population to be 'ageing'?

How can these issues be overcome?

Effect of lockdowns on birth rates in the UK

An article from The Conversation.

By Ann Berrington, Professor of Demography, Centre for Population Change, University of Southampton and Joanne Ellison, Research Fellow, Centre for Population Change, University of Southampton.

Many wondered whether the COVID lockdowns would lead to a baby boom or a bust. We finally have some answers – for the UK, at least.

Broadly, provisional data from the Office for National Statistics suggests there was a temporary decline in babies conceived during the first three months of the first lockdown in 2020, but then the fertility rate rebounded to levels above those seen in previous years. Let's take a closer look.

The earliest we would have expected COVID to affect people's decisions to become pregnant would have been February 2020, influencing births on average from November 2020.

Before the pandemic, the number of births had been falling in all countries of the UK.

By 2019, the average fertility rate for Scotland was 1.37 births per woman. This was the lowest level ever recorded and was significantly lower than the level in 2008 (around 1.77) before the effects of the economic recession hit.

In 2019, fertility rates were slightly higher in England and Wales (1.65) and Northern Ireland (1.82) than in Scotland, but again, these levels were some of the lowest ever recorded.

The onset of the pandemic was initially associated with a decline in the number of births, particularly from November 2020 to February 2021. Yet from March 2021 onward, the number of monthly births recovered and sometimes exceeded 2019 levels, particularly in the last quarter of 2021. This is despite there having been a second wave of the pandemic in the UK in late 2020 and early 2021.

For England and Wales, the average fertility rate in 2021 was 1.61 children per woman compared with 1.58 in 2020 – the first time since 2012 this figure has increased from one year to the next.

This recovery might be explained by births taking place where conception had been postponed during the first lockdown. Or perhaps birth rates had reached their lowest point and would have increased, anyway.

We can find out more about what's happened if we look at trends in birth rates by mother's age. These age-specific fertility rates are, at the time of writing, only published up to 2021 for England and Wales, and are only available for women.

This data shows that the effect of the pandemic on childbearing in England and Wales differed by age. Among women aged under 25, fertility rates fell and continued to fall through 2020 and 2021. Among women in their 30s, fertility rates recovered in 2021 after falling in 2020. Rates for those in their early 40s have remained stable at a low level.

So, what might be happening? In a research article written in 2021, we speculated that the pandemic would not have a uniform effect on fertility rates, but would affect childbearing differently based on a woman's age.

We considered several ways the pandemic might decrease fertility rates. For example, national lockdowns sharply reduced socialising. Young adults may have been particularly affected by this, with fewer opportunities to meet people

Fertility rates by age of mother, England and Wales, 2018-21

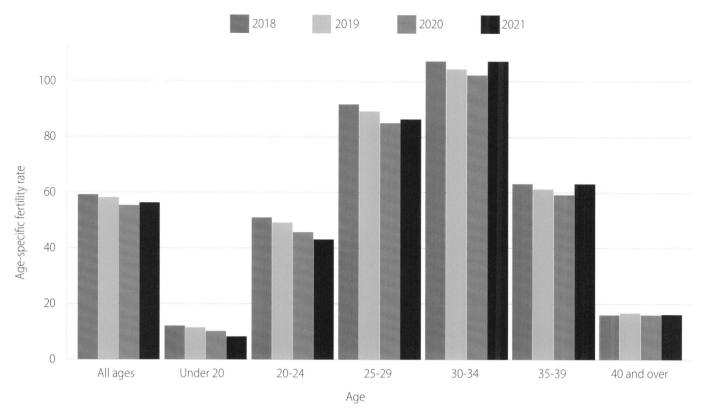

2018 2019 2020 2021

The age-specific fertility rate is measured by the number of live births per 1,000 women in the age group
Source: ONS (2022)

and form romantic and sexual relationships. Meanwhile, increased uncertainties associated with the economic fallout of the pandemic might have deterred people from planning a baby.

We also put forward reasons why the pandemic may increase childbearing, including increased time spent together and a focus on home life among established couples. Furlough and working from home might have encouraged people in longer-term relationships to have children they may not otherwise have had, or that they might have had at a later time. Among parents already considering having another child at some point, births of subsequent children might have been brought forward.

Among younger adults, we found more reasons for a decline in childbearing than an increase, while among slightly older people we found more reasons to expect an increase.

The observed age-specific fertility trends are consistent with our predictions, though from this data we cannot know whether the reasons we proposed were exactly correct.

Looking back and looking forward

Historical evidence on fertility rates following the 2008 recession from other European countries suggests that it is younger people who are most likely to experience a decline in childbearing in response to shocks and crises.

Younger women have more opportunities to postpone their childbearing in response to uncertainties because they have more time to catch up on any births that had previously been put off.

Young people have been uniquely affected by the pandemic, being more likely to lose their jobs, or to change their living arrangements, often returning to their parents' home. Among slightly older women, the pandemic could have increased fertility, for example, through more time spent with their partner, and changes in work-life balance due to COVID.

So what might the future hold in terms of fertility in the UK? Will the increasing birth rates among those in their 30s continue, with previously postponed births caught up at later ages? If this happens, we could see an increase in fertility rates.

Or is the pandemic bounce-back in childbearing a blip in an otherwise downward trend in fertility? Increased economic uncertainty, difficulties in securing stable, affordable housing, a greater awareness of environmental concerns and worries about global security are all likely to diminish certain people's desires to have children.

Ultimately, it will be some years before we know whether the pandemic's effects on childbearing are temporary or will be longer lasting.

21 April 2022

To breed or not to breed? That may be the question

By John Humphrys

In a week when the political drama played out in Westminster has thrown every other news story off the front pages, it might seem perverse to suggest that there is other stuff happening out there that might be worth our attention. But there is. There always is. It's just that the news business craves immediacy, high drama and colourful characters with a whiff of sulphur about them. The issue that I'm seeking your views on this week has none of that but its long-term significance far outweighs what the great Robin Day memorably described as 'here today... gone tomorrow' politicians. It's about children: why we're not having enough of them and what the politicians might consider doing about it.

You'd never have guessed it from the latest census figures, which show that the population of England and Wales is higher than it has ever been at nearly 60 million, but many demographers believe we are entering a population crisis. There are two obvious reasons why a nation's population might be growing and both apply to our country. One is immigration. The other is that we are living so much longer. The biggest growth by far is in the number of those aged between 70 and 74. The second biggest is those over the age of 90. The drop is in the number being born. That may not matter too much right now, but all those ancients (like me) are going to need youngsters coming up behind them. Not just to care for us when we can no longer care for ourselves, but to earn the money and pay the taxes to keep the nation's wheels turning.

It doesn't take a genius to identify at least one of the reasons behind the baby shortage. I was 21 when I got married way back in the sixties. Two years later I was offered a mortgage by the bank and bought a very pleasant new-build house which cost rather less than three times my salary and we started having children. My wife, who was a nurse, gave up her job six months into her pregnancy. All that was pretty common in those far-off days. Now fast forward a few decades.

My youngest son is 22. Ask him or any of his friends when/if they're planning to marry, buy a house, have kids and they'll look at you as if you'd asked them when they planned to win the Nobel Prize for physics or win the Lottery. It's simply not on their horizon. Maybe in their mid-thirties? Maybe never?

But let's assume they do take the plunge and manage to buy a house or (more likely) a flat. Or, even more likely if they live in a big city like London, rent somewhere to live. They'd like to start a family but that would mean one of them giving up their job or paying for child care and they just can't afford it. Hence what many regard as the main reason for the steep fall in the number of births.

Here's what my old colleague Jenni Murray wrote in the *Mail* this week: 'If I were in my early thirties now, would I be planning my first baby? To be honest I doubt it. So many women are choosing not to have children before they are 30 and a significant number still don't have them by 45. Is it any wonder? Who would want to have kids if you can't afford to buy or rent a house, are loaded with student debt and can't see how you'll be able to afford the eye-watering nursery costs needed to keep working?'

One of the reasons it's so expensive is that there is a legal limit of four on the number of two-year-olds who can be looked after by one nursery worker. In London it costs around £85 a day for a two-year-old to attend nursery, which adds up to around £1,700 a month. This week the Government announced the limit will be increased to five. Parents could save £480 a year - assuming the nurseries pass on the savings. But critics say that doesn't go nearly far enough. They point out that British parents pay the third highest childcare costs in the world after Switzerland and Slovakia. The share of net household income spent on childcare is 30 per cent. In Finland it's 18 per cent, and in Denmark just 9 per cent.

Dame Jenni is not alone in pointing to Scandinavian countries like Sweden partly because 'too often, in this country, men are reluctant to take paternity leave, and employers find mothers are afraid to take on a full-time job.' In Sweden, by contrast, employers must offer 16 months of leave which can be shared between both parents. There is, she says, 'a cultural assumption there that both men and women want a work and a family life. And If a child is sick, either parent is entitled to take time off with 80 per cent of their salary.'

But Murray would go further. Much further. She is one of a growing number of mothers who want to do away with the concept of 'childcare' altogether and replace it with free state education which would start from the age of one. She concedes that it's a radical concept but it's 'the only way we can get women back into the workforce, engaged in society, getting equal treatment at work and paying tax.'

There are many other less radical ideas out there. A private members' bill has just been introduced in the House of Lords by Lord Farmer which would allow parents to choose when and how they receive child benefit. Parents could draw more cash in the early years to help pay for nursery places and take less when their teenagers are in school.

The demographer Paul Morland has just published a book highlighting Britain's impending population crisis. He suggests two goals should be set: First, the UK should aim to have a population that is growing moderately. This will meet objections from the 'overcrowded island' lobby even though – as he points out - the UK is far from 'full up'. Only 6 per cent of land is classified as developed. He says that for a healthy economy and for provision of the services we require — from tanker drivers to care-home assistants — we do need a steady rise in the number of workers, at least to do the tasks robots may never master.

His second goal is a 'grow our own' policy. He writes: 'This would aim to provide most of the population growth from births within our racially and ethnically diverse country rather than immigration. Nearly 30 per cent of births in the UK are now to mothers born overseas — like mine, born in Germany. There will always be a place for some immigration, but we should not be as reliant on it as we have been over the past 20 or 30 years. Plus, many of the countries we might get immigrants from are suffering from the same shortage of working-age people.'

Some of his suggestions for how to meet those goals have been mocked by columnists like Alice Thomson of *The Times*. One of the suggestions was a national day to celebrate parenthood. Another was having the monarch send you a congratulatory telegram if you have three babies. If you have none, you might be punished by the tax man. Thomson asked her female readers: 'Have you understood? You are here for a reason. All that talk about studying science was not to become engineers or discover vaccines but so you could have progeny. Get with the birthing programme, ladies. Don't leave it too late. Tick tock!'

Zoe Williams of *The Guardian* was pretty scathing about the 'negative child benefit' too. She described it as 'childless couples paying more tax, to atone for their failure to provide the next generation of bin collectors.' And she asked: 'What if they had been parents, but had been bereaved? How to explain to people who are already contributing more than the value of what they take out of the system that actually they should contribute even more? How to sidestep the implications for homosexuals, who are likely to have fewer, or zero, children? All those questions can be distilled to one: what fresh hell is this? Is it not enough that we're supposed to be constantly at war, generation against generation, region against region, but now we have to do breeders v the rest?'

Where do you stand in all this? Does it worry you that we are not producing enough 'home-grown' babies? Are you one of those who would like to start a family but simply can't afford to and, if so, what do you think the government should do to help you? Or maybe you think we should emulate the American who was boasting this week that he has done his bit 'to help solve the global crisis of falling birth rates' by fathering no fewer than nine children? Just one caveat: his name is Elon Musk and he's the richest man on the planet!

8 July 2022

Discuss

In small groups, discuss and make notes on what you know about changing populations. Consider the following:

- What factors contribute to population growth.
- Is population growth a good thing or a bad thing?
- What is happening to the global population right now?

Will the Caribbean community survive population decline?

Low birth rates, more mixed relationships, and the elderly joining their ancestors are all contributing to fall in census numbers.

By Leah Mahon

The Caribbean community in Britain has faced a sharp decline in numbers, while African communities have surged, prompting fears that Caribbeans could eventually 'vanish'.

The Caribbean community were the only ethnic group to show a decline in the recent population census, with experts suggesting this could be because of low birth rates, more mixed relationships, and the older generation returning to the islands.

To understand the rise and fall in Britain's Caribbean population, a good place to start is history.

More than 100 years before the Empire Windrush landed, black people had already formed a presence in Britain during the Roman conquest period, but most notably between the 16th-18th century.

The Tudor and Stuart eras saw a significant presence of Africans in London, many of them freed slaves and some revolutionary abolitionists.

But several generations later this community had apparently disappeared, as mixed relationships quickly eradicated melanin and culture.

After Windrush, the UK's major cities became strongholds for its blossoming Caribbean communities, from Brixton and Notting Hill, to Handsworth, Chapeltown and St Pauls.

Their vibrant culture changed the fabric of British society, influencing popular culture, sport, entertainment and public services.

Britain saw a steep rise in migration from West Africa to the capital in the 1980s, settling in areas like Peckham and Dalston.

The 2021 census, recently released, shows the overall black population makes up 2.4 million (4.0%) people living in England and Wales, a steep rise from the 1.9 million (3.3%) recorded a decade earlier.

However, while the African population has grown to nearly 3% of the population, the Caribbean population has dwindled to just 1%.

Jason Arday, a writer and Professor of Sociology of Education at Glasgow University, agreed that the reasons are not certain, but the 'globalisation of Africans' has been huge, first from Nigeria and Ghana and then from Somalia.

He told The Voice: 'Over the last 10 to 15 years, primarily led by educational opportunities in education, there's been a huge increase in the number of Africans coming to the UK, particularly with asylum seekers and refugees. By and large people are also seeking out better opportunities and becoming more socially mobile.'

Prof Arday noted that Africans might be more likely to identify as African – and reject 'Britishness' – rather than tick black British on the form.

'A lot of people identify themselves as black African, even though they may be British in the literal sense of the word,' he explains.

'That has also meant the number in terms of Africans could be skewed purely because people are reclaiming some of their identity, and rejecting this notion of Britishness, instead of saying, 'black or black British,' they are determining themselves as Africans.'

An increasing 'Blaxit' trend of black people moving to live and work in the Caribbean, and Africa, could also be contributing to the census findings.

Blaxit can also be seen in the trend to Africanise names, shedding the 'slave name' link, which has accelerated since the xenophobic Brexit campaign.

'People are either leaving these shores as a mode of protection or they are reclaiming some sense of identity in rejecting, imperialistic and kind of empirical views around what it means to be British and the fact that that narrative is only ever constructed by white British people,' Prof Arday adds.

'And as a black or ethnic minority person, if you're not compliant or submissive to that characterisation of what a British person is then I guess what you're told is if you don't like it, you can leave.

Violent

'So a lot of people get to take it upon themselves, if they have the economic means and the social capital, to take themselves out of what's becoming an increasingly violent situation for black people.' The hostile environment, with frequent deportations to Jamaica, and the Windrush scandal could also be the cause for the decline, he suggests.

Louise Owusu-Kwarteng, a Professor in Applied Sociology at the University of Greenwich, says that the 'good immigrant' rhetoric could be adversely impacting Caribbean communities more.

'Nowadays there are very specific ideas about what they see [the government] as a good immigrant and what they see is a bad immigrant,' she told The Voice.

'I wonder whether the long-term stereotyping of African-Caribbean people has played into that and contributes to the general restrictions of people.

'Caribbean people have lived here for longer and so it's taken a while to build up those stereotypes.'

An increasingly elderly cohort within the Caribbean population could also be part of the decline.

The Windrush generation, and some of their children, are joining the ancestors.

Office of National Statistics data shows that from 2007 to 2019, the live birth rate for Caribbeans fell by 26%, a stunning drop. By contrast, African births fell by just 3%.

On top of birth rates dropping, elders passing away, and Blaxit relocations, there is the matter of mixed relationships producing more black mixed heritage children, some of which will go on to be in relationships with white people.

A person with two black parents could have grandchildren who might 'pass for white', and if they have relationships with a white partner, the grandchildren will very probably not be a visible minority.

As some can end up grandparents by their 40's, you can see how quickly this transformation can take place.

2011 census figures show that the mixed heritage population has rocketed, and the most likely group to be in an inter-ethnic relationship overall were white and black Caribbean people by 88%, who were closely followed by 79% of white and black African people.

Inter-ethnic

Mixed or multiple ethnic groups have grown by 3.0% (1.7 million) from the 2.2% (1.2 million) first recorded ten years ago with mixed white and black Caribbean people still being the most popular mixed-race identity in 2021.

Nigel de Noronha, a Research Associate at the University of Manchester, told The Voice: 'It's much more normal for people to be in mixed relations now.

'Overall, there's around two and a half million mixed heritage people in the country. Although mixed [black] Caribbean and white isn't a massive component of that, it's significant in the way that that change has happened.'

The question now is whether the decline in the Caribbean population will continue to decline, or stabilise and increase in the future.

All the indications point to a further decrease, but it may be more difficult to measure in future because the UK government has now discontinued the once-a-decade census.

Given how quickly ethnic groups can disappear over four short generations, some commentators believe the future of the Caribbean community needs to be discussed.

Could the community that gave us the Notting Hill carnival, and whose Caribbean culture has embedded itself into the British way of life eventually fade away?

Today Africans, who in past decades often adopted Caribbean culture, are more proudly African. The Afro-beats movement is proof of that.

However, Prof Arday argues that the contribution of Caribbean people to Britain 'has stood the test of time', and believes the Caribbean and African communities can come closer together.

'The most important thing is what community means, and how we work collectively as a people to really address and penetrate really violent legislations that undermine our egalitarian ideals as black people.

'There's a generation of people coming through that don't identify necessarily as West Indian or African; they identify as black.

'They interfuse the idea as Caribbeans and Africans all being kind of the same thing. And so, that redefining of black means that this generation is working collectively together, that cohesion is slightly different.'

29 December 2022

Advantages and disadvantages of population growth

By Tejvan Pettinger

Over the course of history, the world has seen rapid population growth. It has enabled a rich diversity of culture, technology and improved living standards. However, population growth is increasingly coming at a cost – in particular to the environment. High population levels are contributing to the depletion of natural resources and causing widespread pollution. Some fear population growth is now deeply damaging for both the planet and even the survival of many natural habitats. However, others argue that fears other population growth are misplaced with the planet having room for more people, so long as we learn to live more in harmony with nature and more efficiently in big cities.

Advantages of population growth

1. More people leads to greater human capital. If there are more people, the probability of finding a genius like Einstein, Marie Curie, Beethoven increase. These exceptional people can lead to technological and cultural masterpieces which enrich our lives. The past 200 years have shown exponential growth in technical development and innovation. There are many factors behind this, but the world's growing population means we have a bigger pool of human capital and the possibility of these cutting edge discoveries increases.

2. Higher economic growth. Population growth will lead to economic growth with more people able to produce more goods. It will lead to higher tax revenues which can be spent on public goods, such as health care and environmental projects.

- The obvious evaluation is to say, the crucial thing is not GDP, but GDP per capita. If economic growth is at the same rate as population growth, average living standards will not increase. However, it is possible population growth can also improve per capita incomes. As the population increases, the economy can benefit from a bigger talent pool, economies of scale and greater specialisation. All this can enable higher per capita income, which we have seen in major developed economies.

3. Economies of scale. Farming and industry have been able to benefit from economies of scale, which means as the population grows, food output and manufacturing output have been able to grow even faster than population growth. For example, at the turn of the nineteenth century, Thomas Malthus predicted population growth would lead to famine as we would be unable to feed the growing population. However, his dire predictions failed to materialise because he failed to understand, that the productivity of land, labour and capital could all increase more than proportionately. 300 years ago, most of the population worked on the land. Technological innovation and economies of scale, mean productivity of land has vastly increased as farmers make use of mechanisation and economies of scale for increased food production.

4. The efficiency of higher population density. In terms of per capita carbon footprint, areas with a high population density are significantly more efficient than rural areas and places with a low population. When people live in densely populated areas, they are more likely to use public transport, live in apartment buildings which are easier to heat. In big cities, transport and the delivery of goods is much more efficient, whereas for low population densities, the average cost and environmental footprint are much higher. Therefore, population growth which leads to growth in city conurbations (which is a feature of global growth in the past) is not as environmentally damaging as we may

Population Growth

Pros	Cons
• More scope for innovation, invention and creative genius	• Increased pressures on natural environment
	• Water shortages
• Economies of scale from higher population	• Increases pollution
	• Exacerbates global warming
• Enables specialisation	• More waste creation
	• Congestion
• Higher population densities more efficient	• Over-use of non-renewable resources

Source: www.economicshelp.org

Global population and forecast to 2100

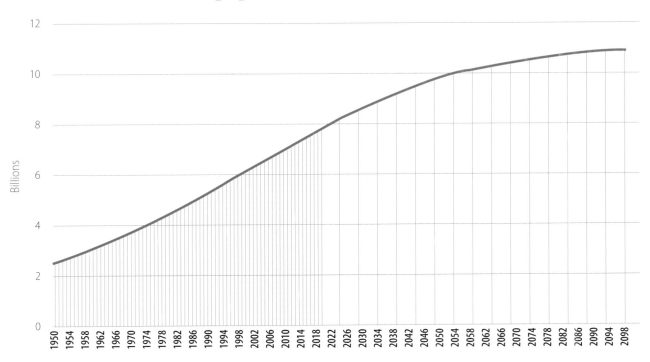

Source: World Bank (1950-20) UN Population forecast 2020-2100

think. In Green Metropolis, by David Owen he argues living in closer proximity in cities is a key aspect of sustainability

- Urban areas account for only 3% of the world's land surface. But, more than 50% of the population. By 2050, the United Nations predict this will rise to 70%. Therefore, population growth doesn't have to lead to an equivalent fall in natural habitats.

5. The improved demographic structure of society. Many western economies are now experiencing a falling population, with the result that their population demographic is being skewed to old, retired people. This is imposing costs on society as we struggle to pay for health care and pensions. Moderate population growth helps to rebalance the population with a higher share of young, working people.

6. Critical mass. Higher populations can enable a critical mass of people to enable a sider, more vibrant society. With low populations, there is less scope for diversity. But, when the population grows, it can enable the support of a broader cultural range of activities.

Disadvantages of population growth

1. Cost to the environment. Population growth exacerbates many of the existing environmental problems

- Trying to reduce carbon and methane emissions to reduce global warming is relatively more difficult as the population grows.

- There will be greater threat on natural habitats as a greater population has greater demand for housing and farmland. This will increase pressure to cut down forests to make way for farming and housing.

- Higher population will lead to a greater consumption of non-renewable resources, leading to a faster depletion of natural resources.

- Higher population will lead to greater pollution levels in air, water and land. Higher pollution is associated with a range of health issues, such as cancer and asthma. The pollution also harms animals and plants.

- Soil degradation. To feed a growing planet, we have seen serious degrading of farmland (according to UN estimates) about 12 million hectares of farmland every year. This is due to factors, such as overgrazing, climate change and use of chemicals.

2. Congestion. Too many people in a small space will lead to various types of congestion. Road congestion is a major problem across the world. One study suggested congestion cost the EU €111 billion (1% of GDP) in 2012. With population growth, the costs of congestion will only increase leading to time lost, more pollution and lost output.

3. Water shortages. Already up to 40% of the world's population face water scarcity and the risk of drought. According to the UN water shortages could lead to 700 million people at the risk of displacement. A growing population will put pressure on scarce water supplies and this is a factor behind many minor and major conflicts with countries having to find ways around the shortage of water.

4. Generating unsustainable waste. We are currently generating non-biodegradable rubbish that we are struggling to process. It tends to end in landfill, causing methane emissions and other toxic problems.

21 November 2021

World Population Prospects 2022: summary of results

Ten key messages

1. The world's population continues to grow, but the pace of growth is slowing down.

In 2020, the growth rate of the global population fell under 1 per cent per year for the first time since 1950. The latest projections by the United Nations suggest that the world's population could grow to around 8.5 billion in 2030 and 9.7 billion in 2050; it is projected to reach a peak of around 10.4 billion people during the 2080s and to remain at that level until 2100. The world's population is projected to reach 8 billion on 15 November 2022, and India is projected to surpass China as the world's most populous country in 2023.

2. Policies aimed at reducing fertility would have little immediate impact on the pace of global growth.

Two-thirds of the projected increase in global population through 2050 will be driven by the momentum of past growth that is embedded in the youthful age structure of the current population. For this reason, further actions by Governments aimed at reducing fertility would not have a major impact on the pace of growth between now and mid-century, beyond the gradual slowdown anticipated by the projections. Nevertheless, the cumulative effect of lower fertility, if maintained over several decades, could be a more substantial reduction of global population growth in the second half of the century.

3. Rapid population growth is both a cause and a consequence of slow progress in development.

Sustained high fertility and rapid population growth present challenges to the achievement of sustainable development. The necessity of educating growing numbers of children and young people, for example, draws resources away from efforts to improve the quality of education. At the same time, achieving the Sustainable Development Goals (SDGs), particularly those related to health, education and gender, is likely to hasten the transition towards lower fertility in countries with continuing high levels.

4. While life expectancy continues to increase globally, large disparities remain.

Population growth is in part caused by declining levels of mortality, as reflected in increased levels of life expectancy at birth. Global life expectancy at birth reached 72.8 years in 2019, an improvement of almost 9 years since 1990. Further reductions in mortality are projected to result in an average global longevity of around 77.2 years in 2050. Yet in 2021, life expectancy for the least developed countries lagged 7 years behind the global average. Similarly, a male disadvantage in life expectancy is observed in all regions and countries, ranging from 7 years in Latin America and the Caribbean to 2.9 years in Australia and New Zealand.

5. A rising share of population in the working ages can help boost economic growth per capita.

In most countries of sub-Saharan Africa, as well as in parts of Asia and Latin America and the Caribbean, the share of population at working ages (between 25 and 64 years) has been increasing thanks to recent reductions in fertility. This shift in the age distribution provides a time-bound opportunity for accelerated economic growth per capita, known as the 'demographic dividend'. To maximize the potential benefits of a favourable age distribution, countries should invest in the further development of their human capital by ensuring access to health care and quality education at all ages and by promoting opportunities for productive employment and decent work.

6. The population of older persons is increasing both in numbers and as a share of the total.

The population above age 65 years is growing more rapidly than the population below that age. As a result, the share of global population at ages 65 and above is projected to rise from 10 per cent in 2022 to 16 per cent in 2050. At that point, it is expected that the number of persons aged 65 years or over worldwide will be more than twice the number of children under age 5 and about the same as the number under age 12. Countries with ageing populations should take steps to adapt public programmes to the growing numbers of older persons, including by establishing universal health care and long-term care systems and by improving the sustainability of social security and pension systems.

7. More and more countries have begun to experience population decline.

Fertility has fallen markedly in recent decades for many countries. Today, two-thirds of the global population lives in a country or area where lifetime fertility is below 2.1 births per woman, roughly the level required for zero growth in the long run for a population with low mortality. The populations of 61 countries or areas are projected to decrease by 1 per cent or more between 2022 and 2050, owing to sustained low levels of fertility and, in some cases, elevated rates of emigration.

8. International migration is having important impacts on population trends for some countries.

For high-income countries between 2000 and 2020, the contribution of international migration to population growth (net inflow of 80.5 million) exceeded the balance of births over deaths (66.2 million). Over the next few

Key Facts

- In 2020, the growth rate of the global population fell under 1 per cent per year for the first time since 1950.

- Global life expectancy at birth reached 72.8 years in 2019, an improvement of almost 9 years since 1990.

- The population above age 65 years is growing more rapidly than the population below that age. As a result, the share of global population at ages 65 and above is projected to rise from 10 per cent in 2022 to 16 per cent in 2050.

- Global life expectancy at birth fell to 71.0 years in 2021, down from 72.8 in 2019, due mostly to the impact of the coronavirus disease (COVID-19) pandemic.

decades, migration will be the sole driver of population growth in high-income countries. By contrast, for the foreseeable future, population increase in low-income and lower-middle-income countries will continue to be driven by an excess of births over deaths. All countries, whether experiencing net inflows or outflows of migrants, should take steps to facilitate orderly, safe, regular and responsible migration, in accordance with SDG target 10.7.

9. The COVID-19 pandemic has affected all three components of population change.

Global life expectancy at birth fell to 71.0 years in 2021, down from 72.8 in 2019, due mostly to the impact of the coronavirus disease (COVID-19) pandemic. Available evidence about the effect of the COVID-19 pandemic on fertility levels remains mixed. In low- and middle-income countries, the availability of and the demand for contraception, as well as reported numbers of unintended pregnancies and births, have remained relatively stable. In high-income countries, where more detailed information is available from birth registration systems, it appears that successive waves of the pandemic may have generated short-term fluctuations in numbers of pregnancies and births. The pandemic severely restricted all forms of human mobility, including international migration.

10. Population data provide critical information for use in development planning.

The COVID-19 pandemic has affected many data collection operations worldwide. Countries and development partners should give priority to the ongoing 2020 round of national population censuses, as such data provide critical information to inform development planning and to assess progress towards the achievement of the SDGs.

July 2022

Prepared by the Population Division of the United Nations Department of Economic and Social Affairs (UN DESA). United Nations, Department of Economic and Social Affairs, Population Division

Child-free by choice: The birth rate crisis gripping the West

With increasing numbers of women rejecting motherhood, governments are left scrambling to try and encourage a baby boom.

By Rosa Silverman

You've slept in, woken up to a tidy home, it's quiet, and you've got the rest of the day to potter around, no interruptions. A child-free life is a good life.' The message floats over a video that captures a scene of serene domesticity. Posted on TikTok a few days ago, it has already racked up more than 100,000 views.

The video's creator, 'Danni "childfree" Duncan', is among those who have helped turn the decision not to have children into something of a movement, complete with its own hashtags (#childfreebychoice and #nothavingkids).

There are thousands of other young women posting similar content, including Nina, who sarcastically challenges the notion that as a #childfreemillennial she's bound to feel 'sad and worthless', while playing a montage of her gloriously child-free travels to make her point. (Trigger warning: such videos are best avoided by exhausted parents in the throes of raising a family.)

It would be easy to dismiss these posts as a social media craze; something young people do to fill their time. Except this craze is just one small part of a wider, and highly significant, demographic issue: across much of the world, birth rates are plummeting.

On Nov 15 this year, the global population is expected to reach eight billion. The United Nations predicts it could grow to about 8.5 billion by 2030 before peaking at 10.4 billion in the 2080s. After that – and some predict it will happen 20 years earlier – the world's population will start to fall.

At a glance, you might conclude the greater cause for alarm is the impending arrival of even more people on our planet. As Population Matters, a UK charity, warns, every additional person increases carbon emissions, not to mention demand on limited food and water resources, and ultimately pressure on borders and social security systems.

But, as averages often do, the headline figures obscure a different story. The few decades of projected global population growth that remain will be driven by a small number of undeveloped countries, many in the Sahel region of Africa. In countries like Niger, which has the world's highest fertility rate, economic conditions remain so harsh that women continue to have an average of six or more children in order to survive.

In contrast, for most of the rest of the world – including Britain – it's a baby bust. And it's happening now. According to the Office for National Statistics (ONS), women born in 1975 had on average just 1.92 children. This compared with the average 2.08 children produced by their mothers' generation (taken as women born in 1949) and is far below the 2.1 children needed for the existing population to replace itself.

The picture is similar in most other developed countries. Last year, the French were urged to have more children after the number of births in the country slumped

Historic population and future UN projections

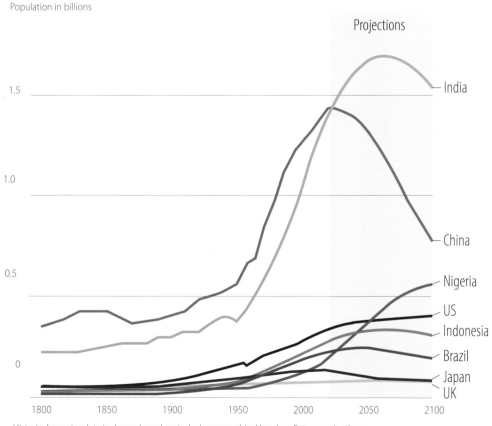

Population in billions

Projections

India
China
Nigeria
US
Indonesia
Brazil
Japan
UK

Historical country data is shown based on today's geographical borders. Future projections are based on the UN's medium-fertility scenario.

Source: Our World In Data

to its lowest level since the Second World War, with 1.83 children born per woman, compared with 2.02 more than a decade earlier. The birth rate in Spain also dropped to a historic low last year, hitting just 1.19 children born to every woman – a 29 per cent fall compared with a decade earlier.

And in parts of Asia the situation is even worse. South Korea's fertility rate sank to its lowest ever in 2020, a meagre 0.84 children per woman, giving the country the lowest birth rate in the world.

So drastic is the decline that populations are expected to halve by 2100 in more than 20 countries, including Spain, Portugal and Japan. Elon Musk, the billionaire Tesla chief executive, has called it 'one of the biggest risks to civilisation'.

But why, when living standards and freedoms have never been higher, are women across the globe having so few children or rejecting the concept of motherhood altogether? And what if anything can policymakers do to reverse the trend?

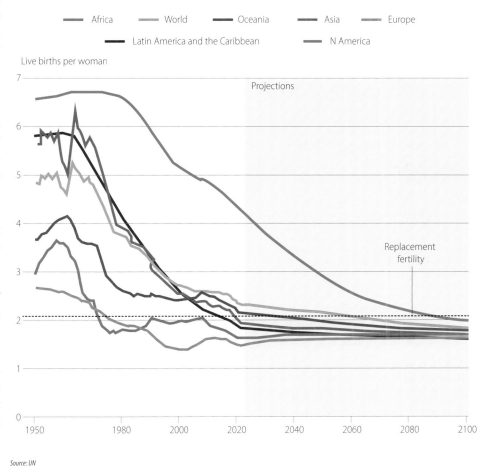

Regional fertility rates

Source: UN

Stresses, strains and changing attitudes

There is no doubt governments are worried. Earlier this month, an unnamed cabinet minister suggested Britain might take its lead from Hungary, where women receive tax cuts for having more children. 'Bonk for Britain' urged the headline in the Sun on Sunday, which quoted the minister saying: 'Look at the labour shortages we are suffering from. We need to have more children. The rate keeps falling.'

It does; but the reasons are many and varied, extending beyond the financial to changing social attitudes and modern lifestyles.

It starts with economics. In undeveloped countries like Niger, where subsistence agriculture dominates, people have large numbers of children to help support the family and look after them in their old age.

But, as countries develop, they all pass a point at which the birth rate begins to fall. It's the point at which it makes more economic sense to invest in the education of just a couple of children. With a doctor or lawyer in the family the future becomes a whole lot more secure.

This typified northern hemisphere countries for the latter part of the last century but, more recently, development appears to have nudged things too far, disincentivising procreation.

In many countries, including Britain, children have become very expensive to raise and, as Professor Geeta Nargund, president of the International Society for Mild Approaches in Assisted Reproduction, wrote in a 2009 paper on declining birth rates in developed countries, 'children often can become an economic drain caused by housing, education cost and other cost[s]'.

The 2007/08 financial crash didn't help. 'Particularly in Europe [this] led to... unemployment [and] poor accumulation of wealth by young adults,' says Lyman Stone, chief information officer at Demographic Intelligence.

Economic stresses and spiralling house prices mean more couples will feel they can't afford children, he explains. Indeed, there is data to suggest that in many countries, including the UK, US, Japan and Germany, couples tend to have fewer children than they would like.

But there's also a complex blend of cultural factors to consider. 'One of the biggest drivers is changing marital trends,' says Stone. 'As people marry later and have children later, that leads to lower fertility.' And among the reasons for later marriage is adults remaining in education for longer, he says. 'People tend not to get married until they have a certain level of stability, and [university] postpones that. As we're creating a society that demands people have more years of [education], we're postponing marriage and so postponing childbirth, and then people may have more difficulties conceiving because they're getting older.'

Attitudes are important too. In the 1950s, as populations in the west boomed, the cult of the nuclear family took hold, with dad diligently working nine-to-five and mum raising the 2.4 children between keeping the house clean with an array of modern gadgets that – allegedly – took the drudgery out of housework. But we live in a different world now and Stone cites a trio of modern attitudes that work against parenthood.

One is high-intensity parenting – which involves investing much time and money into each child. This 'Tiger Mother' version of raising children puts prospective parents off, says Stone.

'We've made parenting very hard these days,' he says. 'It's treated like a research project: you have to read all these books, not feed them this, do feed them that. Parenting anxiety is a real reason people don't have kids. They think parenting is really hard.'

Then there's the rise of 'leisurism' – lifestyles focused on leisure pursuits. In some of its surveys, Demographic Intelligence has asked respondents to agree or disagree with statements like 'I'm working on myself right now', 'my hobbies are important to me' and 'I want to have extra money so I can travel'.

'We find a considerable share of people have leisurist mindsets,' says Stone, 'so it's very important to them to have a lot of leisure time, and time to focus on their own wellbeing and development. We find that with people who have these views, it negatively affects their fertility, meaning they desire fewer children and don't even have as many children as they desire.'

The reverse of the leisurist coin is the 'workist' mindset, in which you value your job very highly as a source of meaning and purpose in your life. Like leisurism, it is not hugely compatible with parenthood. More than one study has suggested a correlation between workist attitudes – which Stone says are prevalent among a growing share of adults – and lower fertility.

But it's not just that the 1950s ideal of family life is fading. Today there is a fast-growing cohort that actively rejects the idea of having children. They are 'childfree by choice', and proud of it.

A survey last year by the Pew Research Center in the US found a rising share of childless American adults said they were unlikely to ever start a family. Some 44 per cent of non-parents aged 18 to 49 fell into this category, up from 37 per cent in 2018. While some cited financial reasons, climate change or their lack of a partner as a reason, the majority (56 per cent) said they probably wouldn't have children because they just didn't want to.

It's a group that's becoming more vocal. In 2015 and 2017, the NotMom Summit – billed as one of the world's first major conferences for women without children – was held in Cleveland, Ohio. In 2021, Erin Spurling, a British woman in her mid-30s, created the Childfree Lounge, an online community for women without children. 'Having children should be a choice, not something you do because everyone else thinks you should,' she told The Daily Telegraph after launching.

It's not hard to find other British women who feel the same. 'I've never wanted children and never wavered from that,' says Beth McCloughlin, 45, a copywriter from south-east London. 'I love my freedom, spontaneity and peace and quiet. I value time alone. I have a low tolerance of routine and mundane tasks.'

She echoes the frustration felt by many like her, at being asked to explain herself for straying from the default expectation for women. 'When people ask me if I never wanted children and why, I feel like they'd just asked me why

I've never chosen to be an astronaut or move to Iraq. I simply never felt the urge to do so and tolerate the sacrifices.'

Gail Hugman from Leigh-on-Sea in Essex, founder of education business Lessons Alive, always knew she didn't want her own children. 'Every "childbearing year" of my life, I would ask myself if I was sure about the decision,' she says. 'And in fleeting moments of regret, I know in my heart it was the right one.'

Pronatal planning

Policymakers beg to differ. Worried by demographic headwinds, a number of countries have launched 'pronatalist' initiatives. These are often financial in nature, such as the family allowance offered by the French state to families with at least two children under 20 (the amount of which varies by income), or the tax exemption for mothers of four or more in Hungary.

Poland's Family 500+ programme offers parents a tax-free benefit of 500 Polish zloty (£91) per month for their second and any subsequent children. In Seoul, South Korea, pregnant women receive rewards of 700,000 won (£436) in transportation vouchers. Singapore, facing a steep decline in its birth rate, has even tried matchmaking couples in the hope of socially engineering a baby boom.

Other pronatalist policies focus on childcare provision and parental leave, with the Nordic nations often praised for their generous support. In Sweden, every pre-school child is entitled to childcare from age one, the cost of which is capped. In Norway, the maximum price for kindergarten is 3,050 kroner (£255) a month. In London, by contrast, it is not unusual to pay upwards of £1,000 a month for a private nursery.

Given British childcare is among the most expensive in the world, costs here inevitably affect family planning. Recent research by Pregnant Then Screwed, a charity aimed at 'ending pregnancy and maternity discrimination', found almost one in five women who had had an abortion cited childcare prices as the main reason.

Thus far, British policies have not exactly screamed 'please have more children'. In 2017, the Conservative government introduced a two-child limit that restricted some benefit payments to the first two children born to the poorest households. Child benefits are also tapered if the higher earning parent makes more than £50,000, and removed completely if they earn above £60,000.

Given the UK's population is on course to peak at 75 million in 2063 and predicted to fall to 71 million by 2100, is it time we followed the lead of other countries in adopting a pronatal approach? The reality is that initiatives elsewhere have had a limited effect. Birth rates are still falling. Following the introduction of Poland's 500+ scheme in 2016, they did rise, but not enough to offset the problems of an ageing population.

Pronatalist policies, moreover, raise some uneasy questions: should the state really have a role in influencing women's decisions about their bodies? Doesn't it have touches of *Brave New World* or *The Handmaid's Tale*? And do such policies even have racist overtones? There was, you'll recall, a party in the 1930s that wanted to increase indigenous births to grow its so-called 'Aryan' population.

But countries with shrinking working populations start to rely on immigration – and this brings problems of its own.

Today, some on the Far Right subscribe to the 'great replacement theory' – the ethno-nationalist idea that white populations are being supplanted by non-white immigrants. Extremists like Brenton Tarrant, who killed 51 people when he attacked two mosques in New Zealand in 2019, have used it to justify violence.

Any treatment or discussion of the birth-rate problem requires, then, a sensitive and careful approach. Introducing pronatalist policies worth having for their own sake, aside from their possible effect on procreation, could be a way forward.

'In general it's good to provide broad structural support for child-rearing, such as a generous child allowance,' says Stone. '[And] we need to make sure housing is affordable.' There may even be positives, with technology allowing societies to exist with fewer workers and less stress being placed on the environment. In his recent book *Decline and Prosper! – Changing Global Birth Rates and the Advantages of Fewer Children*, demographic expert Vegard Skirbekk presents the baby bust as a positive overall. We must, he argues, ultimately adapt to a world with fewer children.

22 October 2022

Key Facts

- According to the Office for National Statistics (ONS), women born in 1975 had on average just 1.92 children. This compared with the average 2.08 children produced by their mothers' generation (taken as women born in 1949) and is far below the 2.1 children needed for the existing population to replace itself.

- South Korea's fertility rate sank to its lowest ever in 2020, a meagre 0.84 children per woman, giving the country the lowest birth rate in the world.

Design

Imagine you have been commissioned by the government of a country with a declining population to design a poster encouraging people to have more children. What incentives do you think you might be asked to include in your design?

US birth rates are at record lows – even though the number of kids most Americans say they want has held steady

An article from The Conversation.

By Sarah Hayford, Professor of Sociology; Director, Institute for Population Research, The Ohio State University & Karen Benjamin Guzzo, Professor of Sociology and Director of the Carolina Population Center, University of North Carolina at Chapel Hill

Birth rates are falling in the U.S. After the highs of the Baby Boom in the mid-20th century and the lows of the Baby Bust in the 1970s, birth rates were relatively stable for nearly 50 years. But during the Great Recession, from 2007-2009, birth rates declined sharply – and they've kept falling. In 2007, average birth rates were right around 2 children per woman. By 2021, levels had dropped more than 20%, close to the lowest level in a century. Why?

Is this decline because, as some suggest, young people aren't interested in having children? Or are people facing increasing barriers to becoming parents?

We are demographers who study how people make plans for having kids and whether they are able to carry out those intentions.

In a recent study, we analysed how changes in childbearing goals may have contributed to recent declines in birth rates in the United States. Our analysis found that most young people still plan to become parents but are delaying childbearing.

Digging into the demographic data

We were interested in whether people have changed their plans for childbearing over the past few decades. And we knew from other research that the way people think about having children changes as they get older and their

circumstances change. Some people initially think they'll have children, then gradually change their views over time, perhaps because they don't meet the right partner or because they work in demanding fields. Others don't expect to have children at one point but later find themselves desiring to have children or, sometimes, unexpectedly pregnant.

So we needed to analyse both changes over time – comparing young people now to those in the past – and changes across the life course – comparing a group of people at different ages. No single data set contains enough information to make both of those comparisons, so we combined information from multiple surveys.

Since the 1970s, the National Surveys of Family Growth, a federal survey run by the National Centers for Health Statistics, have been asking people about their childbearing goals and behaviours. The survey doesn't collect data from the same people over time, but it provides a snapshot of the U.S. population about every five years.

Using multiple rounds of the survey, we are able to track what's happening, on average, among people born around the same time – what demographers call a 'cohort' – as they pass through their childbearing years.

For this study, we looked at 13 cohorts of women and 10 cohorts of men born between the 1960s and the 2000s. We

50 years of births in the US

This figure shows the downward trend in births in the U.S. as measured by the total fertility rate, a commonly used metric that describes the number of births that a hypothetical woman would have over a lifetime, based on age-specific birth rates in a given year.

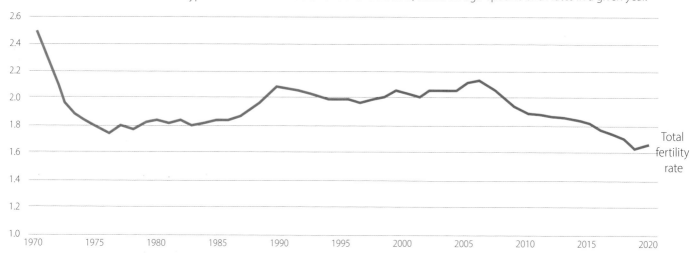

Source: Osterman et al. "Births: Final Data for 2020" National Vital Statistics Reports Feb.7,2022

Planned number of children has held steady

Over half a century of surveys, female teenagers age 15-19 have been fairly consistent, reporting their intention to have an average of just over two children during their lifetime. Each point describes the stated intention of girls born within that five-year period.

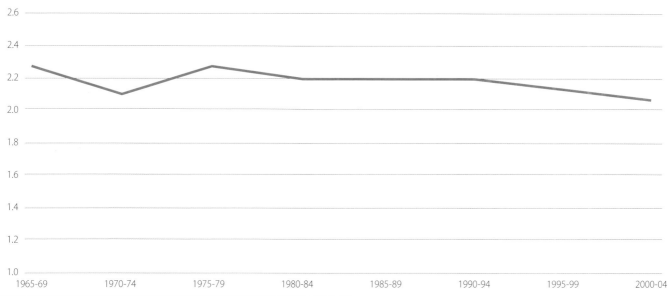

Source: Guzzo and Hayford, "Evolving Fertility Goals and Behaviours in Current U.S. Childbearing Cohorts," Population and Development Review 2023.

followed these cohorts to track whether members intended to have any children and the average number of children they intended, starting at age 15 and going up to the most recent data collected through 2019.

We found remarkable consistency in childbearing goals across cohorts. For example, if we look at teenage girls in the 1980s – the cohort born in 1965-69 – they planned to have 2.2 children on average. Among the same age group in the early 21st century – the cohort born in 1995-1999 – girls intended to have 2.1 children on average. Slightly more young people plan to have no children now than 30 years ago, but still, the vast majority of U.S. young adults plan to have kids: about 88% of teenage girls and 89% of teenage boys.

We also found that as they themselves get older, people plan to have fewer children – but not by much. This pattern was also pretty consistent across cohorts. Among those born in 1975-79, for instance, men and women when they were age 20-24 planned to have an average of 2.3 and 2.5 children, respectively. These averages fell slightly, to 2.1 children for men and 2.2 children for women, by the time respondents were 35-39. Still, overwhelmingly, most Americans plan to have children, and the average intended number of children is right around 2.

So, if childbearing goals haven't changed much, why are birth rates declining?

What keeps people from their target family size?

Our study can't directly address why birth rates are going down, but we can propose some explanations based on other research.

In part, this decline is good news. There are fewer unintended births than there were 30 years ago, a decrease linked to increasing use of effective contraceptive methods like IUDs and implants and improved insurance coverage from the Affordable Care Act.

Compared with earlier eras, people today start having their children later. These delays also contribute to declining birth rates: Because people start later, they have less time to meet their childbearing goals before they reach biological or social age limits for having kids. As people wait longer to start having children, they are also more likely to change their minds about parenting.

But why are people getting a later start on having kids? We hypothesize that Americans see parenthood as harder to manage than they might have in the past.

Although the U.S. economy overall recovered after the Great Recession, many young people, in particular, feel uncertain about their ability to achieve some of the things they see as necessary for having children – including a good job, a stable relationship and safe, affordable housing.

At the same time, the costs of raising children – from child care and housing to college education – are rising. And parents may feel more pressure to live up to high-intensive parenting standards and prepare their children for an uncertain world.

And while our data doesn't cover the last three years, the COVID-19 pandemic may have increased feelings of instability by exposing the lack of support for American parents.

For many parents and would-be parents, the 'right time' to have a child, or have another child, may feel increasingly out of reach – no matter their ideal family size.

12 January 2023

The world is struggling to manage its ageing population

The world's population is ageing. How are we to pay for the pensions and healthcare of a burgeoning number of elderly?

By Bernd Debusmann

Call it baby bust and oldster boom – two trends that signal a demographic transformation without precedent in human history.

In much of the world, declining birth rates and longer life spans are combining to create a phenomenon demographers call global ageing. It brings both problems and opportunities that are hard to fathom and require rethinking the way societies are organized and economies are run.

The world's population of people over 65 is forecast to double by 2050. By that time, a quarter of the people in developed countries will be that age or older. No country has fully figured out how to cope with steadily rising expenditures for the pensions and healthcare of the swelling ranks of senior citizens.

According to United Nations projections, the age group most in need of support – those over 80 – will triple by 2050.

'Unlike other long-term predictions, there is nothing hypothetical about this,' said Richard Jackson, president of the Global Aging Institute, a Washington-based think tank. 'This is as close as social science comes to a certain forecast. Absent a Hollywood catastrophe like a colliding comet or an alien invasion, it will surely happen.'

In China and the U.S., population growth is slowing

The slowing pace of population growth was thrown into sharp focus by data recently released by the world's two biggest economies, the United States and China. And birth rates have been dropping elsewhere, with the exception of sub-Saharan Africa.

In April, the U.S. Census Bureau reported that America's population growth in the past decade slowed to its lowest rate since the 1930s. China, which also conducts a once-in-a-decade census, reported the lowest rate since the 1950s.

The statistics so alarmed the Chinese government that on May 31 it announced that married couples would now be allowed to have three children – a striking reversal from the 'one-child policy' the Communist authorities introduced in 1979 and amended in 2015, when two children were allowed.

Experts view the reversal as an implicit admission that China's decades-long programme of social engineering has failed.

The rationale for restricting the size of families was to ensure that population growth did not outpace economic development in what was then, and still is, the world's most populous country.

Humanity has never faced the challenge of global ageing before

Although global ageing will have a decisive impact on the 21st century, it does not often make headlines. Unlike climate change, global ageing and shrinking population growth have failed to fire the public imagination.

But signs of the trend – fewer babies and longer life spans – have been obvious for years.

One of the demographic milestones that did make headlines came from a Japanese retail number; in 2012, adult diapers for the incontinent elderly began outselling baby diapers. That underscored Japan's status as the country with the world's longest life expectancy – 84.3 years – according to the World Health Organization.

Humanity has never before faced this kind of challenge. 'For most of history, the elderly accounted for a small fraction of the population, never more than 5% in any country,' according to Jackson. That began to change after the 19th century industrial revolution and major achievements in medicine, including a sharp reduction in the number of children dying before their fifth birthday.

In discussions about the end result of the demographic transformation now in progress, two long-range forecasts that proved spectacularly wrong tend to come up.

One was by the 18th century English scholar Thomas Robert Malthus and another by Stanford University professor Paul Ehrlich. Both predicted that population growth would outstrip food supplies and result in world-wide famines.

In 1968, Ehrlich published *The Population Bomb*, a book that said 'hundreds of millions of people are going to starve to death' in the 1970s and urged action to keep birth rates down. The book sold millions of copies and stirred world-wide fears of overpopulation.

World's nations have trouble boosting birth rates, coping with elderly

Since 1968, the world's population has more than doubled. It now stands at 7.9 billion and is still growing, although at a sharply lower rate than in the past. And although there have been famines, mostly in Africa, the world did not run out of food, thanks partly due to innovations in agriculture such as better fertilizers, improved seeds and drip irrigation.

While countries have adapted to the food needs of rising populations, they face problems boosting their birth rates and coping with growing cohorts of the elderly.

Rewards to entice couples to have more children do not appear to be the answer. In Russia, whose current population of 146 million is expected to shrink by 30 million in the next three decades, the government offers cash incentives and washing machines to new parents, but birth rates continue to decline.

'You can't bribe women to have children,' said the GIA's Jackson. In his view, the most important response to fewer

babies and longer life spans would be 'productive ageing' – keeping older people in the work force for longer.

A big obstacle to that in many developed countries is the age – usually 65 – at which government or corporate pensions kick in. The concept of financial support in old age dates back to 1881, when the German statesman Otto von Bismarck introduced it to Germany's Reichstag.

It was originally pegged at 70 years, roughly in line with life expectancy in Germany at the time, and later lowered to 65. America's Social Security Act of 1935 set the retirement age at 65. As Jackson sees it, this is a policy that pushes older workers into premature retirement.

For rich countries, one way to balance the age distribution is to open the door to young immigrants. But with anti-immigrant sentiment running high in much of Europe and the United States, immigration reforms are a thorny issue. It's where, as Jackson put it, 'economic logic collides with politics.'

21 June 2021

Bernd Debusmann began his international career with Reuters in his native Germany and then moved to postings in Eastern Europe, the Middle East, Africa, Latin America and the United States. For years, he covered mostly conflict and war and reported from more than 100 countries. He was shot twice in the course of his work: once covering a night battle in the centre of Beirut and once in an assassination attempt prompted by his reporting on Syria. He now writes from Washington on international affairs.

Three questions to consider

1. Why will global ageing require a rethinking of how economies are run?
2. Do you think your country's government does enough for its elderly population?
3. What do you think is the right age for retirement?

Sustainable Population: Earth4All Approach - Population Matters

Earth4All's recent People and Planet report is the latest attempt at modelling sustainable population projections through the 21st century. It caused a number of exaggerated newspaper headlines, but are its projections of a significant fall in population by 2100 plausible?

The release of a new report caused a bit of a stir at the end of March. *The Guardian*'s headline ran 'World "population bomb" may never go off as feared, finds study', and many people took to Twitter to ask questions along the lines of, 'What were you worried about?'.

While Twitter is probably not your first port of call for reasoned debate and nuanced opinion, just what was all the fuss about?

What is the 'ideal' population size?

The question of what population size is environmentally sustainable has been addressed multiple times. While estimates have ranged from as low as 100 million, the most frequently occurring figure is 2-3 billion. Others have taken a different approach and posed the question of whether a good life could be provided to all within planetary boundaries. They show that while only the basic needs of 7 billion could be met currently, by implementing significant changes in social and technical provisioning systems and shifting consumption towards sufficiency, a good life for the same number of people could be sustained.

All previous interrogations of sustainable population have treated population itself as a factor determined independently of other social and environmental dynamics and have largely relied on the population projections generated by the United Nations Population Division (UNPD).

The Earth4All Analysis

This most recent attempt to address the question of sustainable population comes from the Earth4All (E4A), 'an international initiative to accelerate the systems-change we need for an equitable future on a finite planet'. Specifically, E4A's working paper addresses questions posed by the Swedish non-profit Global Challenges Foundation (GCF) around the number of people that the Earth might sustain at different levels of welfare, changes in technology and resource management.

The E4A explore the GCF's questions under two contrasting scenarios: Too Little Too Late (TLTL), and the Giant Leap. Unlike other attempts that calculate a figure for an environmentally sustainable population and then compare it with separately modelled population projections, the E4A model combines the two.

Too little too late

Running the TLTL model to the end of this century results in a moderate slowing of global population growth with a peak of just under 9 billion reached by mid-century. Similarly, economic growth somewhat slows but average per capita global incomes continue to increase. However, despite population size reaching a considerably lower peak than that projected by the UN, labour participation rates decline, as does trust in government.

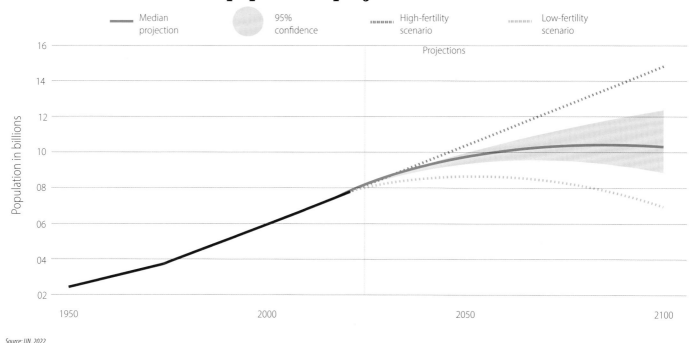

UN population projections to 2100

Source: UN, 2022

Scenario 1:
Too Little Too Late:

What if we continue on our current destructive path?

'This scenario reflects our current trajectory. What if societies continue at a similar pace, setting incremental goals but failing to take strong collective action? Will we cross irreversible tipping points, threatening the foundations of Earth's stable climate? Will skyrocketing inequality lead to worsening social tensions?' – Earth4All

Moreover, inequality and ecological footprint increases are accompanied by huge losses in wildlife. However, while planetary boundaries are further breached with carbon emissions pushing warming to 2.5°C by the end of the century, the TLTL model does not anticipate global climate or ecological collapse.

Despite this, E4A predict that under the TLTL model regional societal collapses increase in the decades leading to 2050 as deepening social division within and between societies increase. In particular, countries with poor governance and high ecological vulnerabilities are most at risk.

Giant leap
In the second scenario, the Giant Leap (GL), E4A sketch out a developmental future where institutions eliminate poverty and substantially reduce the risks from Earth system shocks. Specifically, five key factors are addressed in the GL scenario:

1. end poverty
2. address gross inequality
3. empower women
4. create a food system healthy for people and ecosystems
5. transition to clean energy

Importantly, it is emphasised that...

'These extraordinary turnarounds are designed as policy and investment road maps that will work for the majority

Scenario 2:
The Giant Leap:

What if we achieve the fastest economic transformation in history?

of people. They are not an attempt to create some impossible-to-reach utopia; instead, they are an essential foundation for a resilient civilisation on a planet under extraordinary pressure. The world is increasingly recognising that there are sufficient knowledge, funds and technologies in the world to implement them.' –People and Planet, pg. 20

However, the GL is optimistic. Under this scenario global population peaks at 8.5 billion in 2040 and declines to 6 billion by 2100. Greenhouse gases continuously fall reaching 90% of their 2020 level by 2050 and global warming is kept below 2°C above preindustrial levels.

'This scenario assumes societies embark on a new path to a sustainable world by 2050. What if we fundamentally reconfigure our economies, energy and food systems so that they work for both people and the planet? Can we avoid the worst of climate change impacts and increase our societies' resilience to shocks? Will we succeed in ending extreme poverty, guaranteeing everyone a healthy diet and access to quality education and healthcare?' – Earth4All

Human wellbeing improves considerably under the GL scenario with inequality slowly declining and incomes increasing. All of these improvements are the outcome of significant interventions both within nation-states and between them. To achieve all five turnarounds in the Great Leap scenario, E4A calculate that 2-4% of global GDP will need to be deployed. While this might be obtained via methods such as borrowing or increasing the money supply, E4A advocate increasing taxes for the richest 10% of the global population by between 4-8%.

A question of models

In terms of future population growth under both scenarios, the historically demonstrable negative relationship between birth rates and GDP forms the 'causal bedrock' of the E4A model. While acknowledging the multiple factors which affect birth rates, the report argues that GDP can be understood as a proxy for key factors such as education, access to contraception and socio-economic mobility.

Economic growth in low-income countries thus becomes a critical factor in the lowering of birth rates. The authors of the report are aware that their approach is not without difficulties and acknowledge where they have made assumptions.

The simple historical correlation between GDP and fertility reduction is therefore primarily deployed in the interests of modelling simplicity, but the E4A team acknowledge elsewhere the importance of policy interventions specifically aimed at reducing fertility through the improvement of women's opportunities via provision of education, health and contraception amongst other measures.

The report's authors are not shy about pinning their own particular colours to the mast when they argue:

> 'According to our results across all simulations for both scenarios, the primary issue is not overpopulation in comparison with available resources, but rather the current (too) high consumption levels among the world's richest quarter. Or, put even more concisely: humanity's main problem is distribution rather than population.'–
> People and Planet, pg. 34

Yet, despite this appearing to be entirely inconsistent with research by work by O'Neill et al. (2018) who clearly show that distribution alone cannot provide a good life to all, the conclusion must be viewed within the context of the model.

E4A's modelling under the GL scenario does not pursue an equal shares approach but attempts to argue for a concerted but gradual transition towards reducing global inequality with the result being the meeting of many of the key social and economic conditions, such as women's empowerment, education and access to family planning, which lead to lower levels of fertility. The model itself does not focus on lowering fertility per se, rather lower fertility is an unintended consequence of tackling poverty with particular progressive policies.

Are the E4A population projections realistic?

As noted above, in the TLTL scenario it is unclear whether climate change has a significant effect on mortality and hence peak population size. Whether this is the case or not, E4A clearly regarded TLTL as the least desirable approach producing the greatest risks in terms of welfare and the stability of the Earth system.

The more desirable GL scenario reduces fertility at a considerable pace as the developmental goals of the model are met, and whether this is considered overly optimistic, the outcome is similar to other models where meeting the contraceptive and education aspirations of the SDGs predicted a population size of 6.29 billion by 2100.

3 May 2023

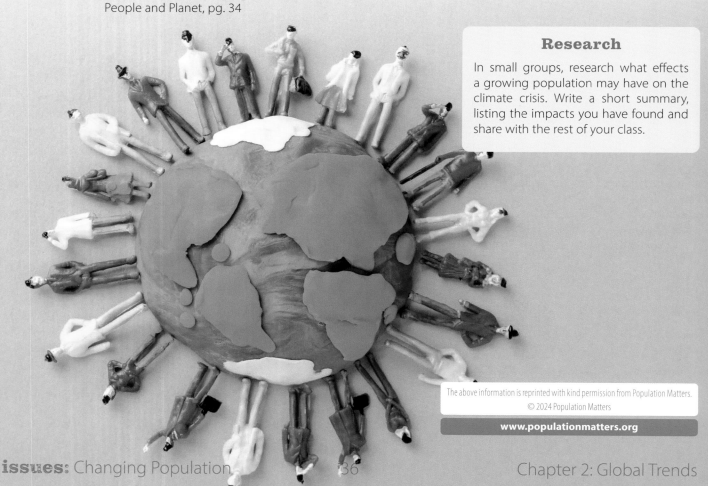

Research

In small groups, research what effects a growing population may have on the climate crisis. Write a short summary, listing the impacts you have found and share with the rest of your class.

Why is nobody willing to say the 'P' word?

Population growth is one of the top two drivers of climate and ecological destruction, writes Donnachadh McCarthy.

With extraordinarily apt timing, the terrifying global 'eight billion people day' arrived in the middle of the failed Cop27 in Egypt. It came just 11 years after the previous 'seven billion day' in 2011. And the UN predicts we will pass 10 billion day by 2080.

We are adding 80 million to the global population annually. That is just under the population of Britain, Belgium and Ireland combined. All of these people will require land, water and other resources to feed, house, wash, transport, clothe and more. Combined with exploding consumption, the population explosion is pushing humanity over the climate and ecological crises cliffs.

The draft Intergovernmental Panel on Climate Change (IPCC) report in April 2022 stated that 'globally, gross domestic product (GDP) per capita and population growth remained the strongest drivers of CO_2 emissions from fossil fuel combustion in the last decade'.

Between 2010 and 2019, growth in GDP per capita raised emissions by 2.3 per cent annually and population growth raised emissions by 1.2 per cent a year. So why is there a deathly silence from the climate movement and at Cop on the 'P' word?

The issue is a minefield due to past authoritarian crackdowns on women's fertility in countries such as India and China, and because a minority on the left scream 'eco-fascism' the moment it is mentioned.

But the solution to the population crisis is one that all NGOs can support. It is simply to ensure that all women have a universal right to voluntary family planning, education and economic independence.

When women are empowered, fertility rates dive to replacement rates or below. This would help to reverse the ecological destruction wreaked since 1900, when the human population was just 1.5 billion.

The main opponents of such rights are patriarchal religions and, increasingly in the global North, nativist populists.

These include those in the US, Hungary and Poland, where women's reproductive rights are targeted by the populist, racist far-right.

Donald Trump cut off US funding of the United Nations Population Fund (UNFPA), the UN body promoting access for women to voluntary family planning. But the Sunak/Johnson government followed Trump with a devastating 85 per cent cut.

To mark 'eight billion day', we asked political parties and leading environmental NGOs two questions: 'The IPCC says global GDP per capita and population growth are the strongest drivers of CO_2 emissions. What actions do you think the government should take?' And: 'Do you back a reversal of the UK funding cut to the UNFPA?'

Of those that answered, all omitted the 'P' word, with the exception of Friends of the Earth, which called it a distraction. It told us: 'The main drivers of environmental destruction and climate breakdown are overconsumption and demand for energy. Focusing on population growth distracts from the need for action by rich countries to cut emissions.' But it did positively state that it was against all aid cuts, without mentioning the UNFPA.

FoE added: 'A sustainable society is about more than fairer shares of resources – it's about sharing power, protecting rights and freedoms. All women and girls should have equal access to reproductive healthcare, which is a fundamental human right.'

Its website has a bizarre policy stating: 'No reliable scientific estimates of sustainable human population size exist, and such estimates would be provisional and technology-dependent. Only focusing on population growth is not the most effective or just approach.' But nobody says that population is the only thing that needs to be addressed.

The problem is the opposite: almost nobody is advocating action on one of the top two drivers of climate and ecological destruction.

Positively, Greenpeace did support the call to reverse the UK cut to the UNFPA, but was at pains to say this was due to support for women's rights, rather than any impact it has on population.

It said: 'Giving women control over their reproductive cycle is crucial to their wellbeing and their communities. We urge the UK government to rethink its cuts to the UNFPA. We support women's reproductive rights on their own merits, not just as a means to an end.'

The only environmental NGO that addressed the IPCC report's findings on both GDP and population was Population Matters, whose patrons include David Attenborough, Jane Goodall & Partha Dasgupta.

Chief executive Robin Maynard told us: 'The UNFPA cuts are devastating, showing indifference to the world's poorest. Two-hundred and seventy million women worldwide lack access to or choice over safe family planning – a basic human right. Cruelly, the cuts mean millions more unintended pregnancies and "back-street" abortions, and thousands more maternal deaths.'

Maynard added: 'Universal access to family planning and education for girls, according to Project Drawdown, would save more emissions than all offshore and onshore wind power combined.'

The WWF reply omitted any reference to population, choosing instead to urge more action by the UK government on emissions. Labour failed to provide any reply.

The Lib Dems did reply, saying: 'UK foreign aid is a matter of life and death. The government callously refuses to recognise this and the cuts to UNFPA are yet another example. Women's rights remain under attack globally and the government is abandoning them.' Again, they left out the 'P' word.

Since 1975, our global population has doubled from four billion to eight billion, and carbon emissions have more than doubled from 17 billion tons of CO2 per annum to 37 billion tons per annum.

As our numbers have exploded, we have destroyed more than 70 per cent of our fellow species' populations since 1970. Millions of women and men all over the world are already limiting family sizes as they realise the existential destructiveness of the population explosion. So please email your Tory or Labour MP and demand they support restoration of the UNFPA funding, so that all women have the right to voluntarily do the same.

23 November 2022

Key Facts

- The Day of Eight Billion, marked on 15 November 2022, was designated by the United Nations as the approximate day when the world population reached eight billion people.

- Since 1975, our global population has doubled from four billion to eight billion, and carbon emissions have more than doubled from 17 billion tons of CO2 per annum to 37 billion tons per annum.

Estimates suggest population growth rate to peak at 8.6 billion

A new projection of the population growth rate highlights that the world's population could peak at 8.5 billion people by 2050, and decline to 7 billion in 2100

While significantly lower than several prominent population estimates, including those of the United Nations, researchers from the Earth4All initiative for the Global Challenges Foundation used a new system dynamics model to understand the population growth rate.

Exploring two scenarios this century, researchers entail that investment into economic development, education, and health could help the global population growth rate to peak at 8.5 billion people by 2050.

Some argue that this decline in population size would be beneficial, as larger population sizes lead to greater consumption of non-renewable resources, leading to a faster depletion of natural resources, as well as greater pollution levels in air, water and land.

However, researchers suggest new models which counteract this belief.

Investment in poverty alleviation could aid population issues

The research looks across ten regions such as Sub-Saharan Africa, China, and the United States. Currently, population growth is highest in some nations in Africa, such as Angola, Niger, the Democratic Republic of Congo and Nigeria, and Asia, for example, Afghanistan.

The first scenario the researchers propose is titled 'Too Little Too Late'. It follows the trend that the world continues to develop economically in a similar way to the last 50 years.

The model suggests that within this trend, most of the very poorest countries break free from extreme poverty,

to which, researchers estimate the global population could peak at 8.6 in 2050 before declining to 7 billion in 2100.

Particular investment in education and health could end extreme poverty by 2060

In the second scenario, called the 'Giant Leap', an unprecedented investment in poverty alleviation, particularly investment in education and health – along with extraordinary policy turnarounds on food and energy security, inequality and gender equity, could end extreme poverty by 2060.

With a marked impact on global population trends, the researchers estimate that in the Giant Leap, the population peaks at 8.5 billion people by around 2040 and declines to around 6 billion people by the end of the century.

Why does economic development or educational attainment matter?

Per Espen Stoknes, Earth4All project lead, said: 'We know rapid economic development in low-income countries has a huge impact on fertility rates. Fertility rates fall as girls get access to education and women are economically empowered and have access to better healthcare.'

Beniamino Callegari, an Associate Professor from Kristiania, added: 'Few prominent models simulate population growth, economic development and their connections simultaneously.

'If we assume these countries adopt successful policies for economic development then we can expect the population to peak sooner rather than later.'

Is the large population growth rate the worst factor, or is it overconsumption?

What is the connection between population and exceeding planetary boundaries? Many argue that the population growth rate is dangerous, as overpopulation leads to fewer resources for many.

However, the researchers discredit this estimation, as they argue the carrying capacity of Earth would be okay – but only without overconsumption from richer nations and bodies.

The carrying capacity of Earth, contrary to public popular myths, suggests that population size is not the prime driver of exceeding planetary boundaries such as climate change. Instead, it is extremely high material footprint levels among the world's richest 10% that are destabilising the planet.

'A good life for all is only possible if the extreme resource use of the wealthy elite is reduced.'

According to the team's demographic projections, the entire population could achieve living conditions exceeding the United Nations minimum level without significant changes in current developmental trends, provided an equal distribution of resources.

At current population levels, it would be possible for everyone to escape extreme poverty and have a life with access to food, shelter, energy and other resources – but only with an equal distribution of resources.

Jorgen Randers, one of the leading modellers for Earth4All and co-author of *The Limits to Growth*, said: 'Humanity's main problem is luxury carbon and biosphere consumption, not population. The places where the population is rising fastest have extremely small environmental footprints per person compared with the places that reached peak populations many decades ago.

'A good life for all is only possible if the extreme resource use of the wealthy elite is reduced.'

27 March 2023

The world's oldest populations

By Felix Richter

- The number of people aged 65 and older is expected to double over the next three decades, reaching 1.6 billion in 2050.

- Asia is leading this trend, with Hong Kong, South Korea and Japan expected to have the highest share of people aged 65 and older by 2050.

- The UN calls population ageing a 'major success story', but says it brings both challenges and opportunities.

- One of the main challenges is ensuring economies can support the consumption needs of a growing number of older people.

As the UN commemorates World Day of Social Justice on February 20, we're taking a look at one of the key challenges the world is facing in the coming decades: the gradual and largely irreversible shift towards an older population. According to the United Nations Population Division, the number of persons aged 65 and older is expected to double over the next three decades, reaching 1.6 billion in 2050.

As the following chart shows, Asia is at the forefront of this trend, with Hong Kong, South Korea and Japan expected to have the highest share of people aged 65 and older by 2050. While Japan is famous for its old population and was already topping the list in 2022, other Asian economies are in the middle of a significant shift, as life expectation has rapidly improved over the last decades and continues to do so. By 2050, roughly 40 percent of the populations of Hong Kong, South Korea and Japan are expected to be 65 and older, which makes a huge difference to levels currently observed in highly developed regions, where the share of older people is in the low 20s.

'Population ageing is a defining global trend of our time,' the UN Department for Economic and Social Affairs writes in its World Social Report 2023, calling it a 'major success story' that brings both challenges and opportunities. One of the main challenges for countries with ageing populations is to ensure that the economy can support the consumption needs of a growing number of older people, be it by raising the legal retirement age, removing barriers to voluntary labour force participation of older people or by ensuring equitable access to education, health care and working opportunities throughout the lifespan, which can help to boost economic security at older ages.

Especially countries in the early stages of the demographic shift have the opportunity to plan ahead and implement the right measures ahead of time, to effectively manage the challenges that come with an ageing population.

22 February 2023

The world's oldest populations

Countries/territories with the highest share of people aged 65 and older*

Legend: Europe — Asia — Caribbean

2022

29.9% Japan	
24.1% Italy	
23.3% Finland	
22.9% Puerto Rico	
22.9% Portugal	
22.8% Greece	
22.4% Germany	
22.4% Bulgaria	

2050

Hong Kong 40.6%	
South Korea 39.4%	
Japan 37.5%	
Italy 37.5%	
Spain 36.6%	
Taiwan 35.3%	
Greece 34.5%	
Portugal 34.3%	

Useful Websites

www.capx.co

www.economicshelp.org

www.independent.co.uk

www.migrationobservatory.ox.ac.uk

www.news-decoder.com

www.ons.gov.uk

www.openaccessgovernment.org

www.populationmatters.org

www.telegraph.co.uk

www.theconversation.com

www.theguardian.com

www.un.org

www.weforum.org

www.voice-online.co.uk

www.yougov.co.uk

Further reading

Pages 9-11: https://migrationobservatory.ox.ac.uk/resources/briefings/the-impact-of-migration-on-uk-population-growth/, Accessed 18/09/2023
Children of Men, P.D James
Decline and Prosper! – Changing Global Birth Rates and the Advantages of Fewer Children, Vegard Skirbekk
The Limits to Growth, Donella Meadows, Jorgen Randers
The Population Bomb, Paul R. Ehrlich
Pages 24-25: From UN Population Division, © 2022,United Nations. Reprinted with the permission of the United Nations. https://www.un.org/development/desa/pd/sites/www.un.org.development.desa.pd/files/undesa_pd_2022_wpp_key-messages.pdf date accessed: 18 September 2023.

Glossary

Ageing population

A population whose average age is rising. This can be caused by increased life expectancy, for example following significant medical advances, or by falling birth rates, for example due to the introduction of contraception. However, the higher the proportion of older people within a population, the lower the birth rate will become due to there being fewer people of childbearing age.

Baby boomer

A person who was born following the Second World War, from 1946-1964, when there was a significant increase in the birth rate.

Birth rate

The number of live births within a population over a given period of time, often expressed as the number of births per 1,000 of the population.

Census

A census is a periodic, official count of all people and households. A census takes place every 10 years in the UK.

Death rate

The number of deaths within a population over a given period of time, often expressed as number of deaths per 1,000 of the population.

Demographic changes (ageing population/grey population)

Demographics refer to the structure of a population. We are currently experiencing an increase in our ageing population. People are living longer thanks to advancements in medical treatment and care. Soon, the world will have more older people than children. This means that the need for long-term care is rising.

Demographics

Statistical characteristics of a population: for example, age, race or employment status.

Depopulation

The substantial decline or reduction in the population of an area.

Infant mortality rate

The number of infant deaths (infants are usually defined as one year old or younger) per 1,000 live births of the population.

Life expectancy

The average period that a person may be expected to live.

Natural change

Natural change is the number of births minus the number of deaths.

Overpopulation

Overpopulation is when an area's population exceeds the capacity of the environment to support it to an acceptable standard of living.

Population growth

An increase in the number of people who inhabit a specific region. This is caused by a higher birth rate and net immigration than the death rate and net emigration. Since the start of the 20th century the rate of global population growth has increased drastically, growing from just 1.6 billion at the turn of the 20th century to eight billion today.

Sustainable population

A population which has enough natural resources within its environment to thrive, but uses them in a manner which allows for them to be constantly renewed and replaced, thereby ensuring that resources will be available to future generations.

Index

A
African people in Britain 20–21
ageing population
    economic impacts 15
    global 25, 32–33, 41
    UK 2–3, 4–7

B
birth rates
    economic growth and 26–27, 36
    global 26–29
    population estimates 8–9
    pronatal policies 29, 33
    UK 12–13, 16–17
    United States 30–31
Blaxit 20–21

C
Caribbean community, UK 20–21
census, UK 1, 2–3, 4, 6–7
childbearing goals 18–19, 26–29, 30–31
childcare 19, 29
coastal areas 7
COVID 16–17, 25

D
data, uses of 4, 6–7, 25
death rates 8
decline, population 14–15, 25, 39
density, population 14–15, 22–23
diversity 5

E
economic growth 35–36, 39
economic impacts
    effect on childbearing 26–27, 29, 31
    of population change 12–13, 14–15,
      22–23, 24
England 1, 10
environmental impacts 12–13, 22–23,
  35, 37–38
estimates, population 8–11, 34

F
fertility rates *see also* birth rates
    global 24–25, 26–27, 36
    UK 8–9, 13, 16–17

G
'Giant Leap' 35–36, 39
growth, population
    benefits of 14–15, 19, 22–23
    global 24
    UK 1–3

H
housing 5

L
life expectancy 24, 25

M
median age, UK 1
migration 8–11, 13, 15, 20–21, 25
mixed ethnic groups 21

N
National Records of Scotland (NRS) 2–3
natural population change 8–9
Northern Ireland 1, 10

O
Office for National Statistics (ONS) 1
older people 4–7, 25
overpopulation 14–15, 33

P
pronatal policies 29, 33

R
retirement age 33
rural areas 7, 22

S
Scotland 1, 2–3, 10
sustainable development 24
sustainable population 34–36, 37, 40

T
'Too Little Too Late' 34–35, 36, 39
transport 6

U
United States 30–31
UNPFA (United Nations Population
  Fund) 37–38
urban areas 22–23

W
Wales 1, 10
women, empowering 36, 37–38